JEWELS
OF THE PHARAOHS

CYRIL ALDRED

JEWELS
OF THE PHARAOHS

Egyptian Jewelry of the Dynastic Period

SPECIAL PHOTOGRAPHY IN CAIRO BY
ALBERT SHOUCAIR

100 colour plates

56 monochrome plates

37 text illustrations

PRAEGER PUBLISHERS

NEW YORK · WASHINGTON

BOOKS THAT MATTER

Published in the United States of America in 1971
by Praeger Publishers, Inc., 111 Fourth Avenue,
New York, N.Y. 10003

© 1971 in London, England, by Thames and Hudson Ltd.

All rights reserved

No part of this publication may be reproduced, stored
in a retrieval system or transmitted in any form
or by any means, electronic, mechanical, photocopying,
recording or otherwise, without the prior permission
of the Copyright owner.

Library of Congress Catalog Card Number: 72-108266

Printed in Switzerland

Contents

CHAPTER ONE

The Recovery of Ancient Egyptian Jewellery

On the 22nd day of the 3rd month of the Winter Season, in the 16th regnal year of the Pharaoh Ramesses IX (i.e. *c.* 1124 BC), a certain stonemason, Amun-pnufer, was taken in custody to the Treasury of the Temple of Mont, to the north of modern Karnak, and there brought before a tribunal of high officials, presided over by the Vizier, who was investigating allegations of wholesale robbery among the tombs at Western Thebes on the opposite bank of the Nile. After being beaten as a foretaste of what to expect if he withheld information, Amun-pnufer was made to take an oath to speak the truth and repeat evidence he had given three days before at a preliminary examination. While the secretary of the court took down his testimony, and incidentally preserved it for our eyes to read, Amun-pnufer described how he and seven other members of his gang had taken their mason's tools and forced their way into the tomb of King Sobek-em-saf of the Seventeenth Dynasty who had lived over four centuries earlier. They had eventually reached an inner place where the body of the king lay: and in an adjoining chamber they found the burial of his queen, Nub-kha-es.

'We found the noble mummy of the sacred king,' he went on, 'equipped with a scimitar. Numerous golden amulets and ornaments were upon his breast and a golden mask was over his face. The noble mummy of this king was entirely bedecked with gold and his coffins were embellished with gold and silver, both inside and out, and inlaid with precious stones. We collected the gold, together with the amulets and jewels that were about him and the metal that was on his coffins. We found the queen in the same state and retrieved all that we found upon her. Then we set fire to their coffins. We took the furnishings that we found with them comprising objects of gold, silver and bronze and divided the spoils amongst us . . . amounting to 160 deben [about 14½ kilos] of gold in all.'

Amun-pnufer concluded his confession by admitting that he and his gang had been robbing tombs at Western Thebes during the previous four years, but he sought to justify himself by asserting that a large number of other people did the same and were as good as partners in his crimes.[1]

Near the end of July, AD 1916, Western Thebes was visited by one of the very rare but severe rainstorms that break over the desert and suddenly convert the empty water-courses of the region into roaring torrents even miles from the centre of the disturbance. The raging flood scours out new channels as well as old in its moments of fury and spills over in cascades, washing away detritus and shifting surface deposits as by the spade of the excavator. This phenomenon was well known to the natives of Qurna at Western Thebes who, when the storm had spent its force, roamed over the cliffs of the neighbourhood to see what the floods might have exposed. It was in this way that at the bottom of a cleft among the crags, not an hour's walk from where Amun-pnufer and his confederates had operated three thousand years earlier, one of the gangs found a tomb in which three queens of Tuthmosis III had been laid to rest c. 1480 BC in all their funerary splendour and with a rich complement of toilet objects and vessels in gold and silver, in addition to their crowns and the other jewels they had worn in life. Their coffins had already rotted from damp and it did not take the gang long to rifle the burials and sell the loot to various dealers who soon dispersed it to Europe and America, where the bulk of it now forms one of the treasures of the Metropolitan Museum of Art.[2]

Pls. 61–66, 84–86

These two accounts separated by three millennia of history will serve to show why it is in the nature of a miracle that any ancient Egyptian jewellery should have survived reasonably intact to modern times. The hunt for valuable grave goods in Egypt has gone on relentlessly since a little after the time of the first burial in that land and has entered into its folklore, and into such stories as those of

Aladdin and Ali Baba. The wealth of treasure found in the tomb of Tut-ankh-amun and in those of the later kings at Tanis, has revealed what compelling incentives there were for the impoverished and greedy to risk all in a search for sudden riches. The reason why the mummies of the great Pharaohs of the New Kingdom repose in a despoiled and shattered state in the Cairo Museum is that, by the time the rulers of Thebes in the tenth century BC had rescued their remains, they had suffered miserably from the axes of the more impious and rapacious of their subjects eager to strip them of the jewels with which they were smothered, the only traces of which are now occasional impressions left on their hardened skins. The sole difference between the thieves of Qurna in 1916 and their ancestors in 1124 BC was that in the case of the former, more could be got for their plunder by selling it intact than by melting it down.

Pls. 91–112, 121–124

Pls. 135–140

The special aura that attaches to finds of jewellery in modern Egypt is nowhere better sensed than in the account of the discovery of the jewellery of Queen Ah-hotpe of the early Eighteenth Dynasty (*obit. c.* 1550 BC). In 1859 one of the agents of Auguste Mariette, the Frenchman who had just been appointed Conservator of Monuments by Said Pasha, while excavating in the detritus of the Dra 'Abu l'Naga at Western Thebes, found the coffin of the queen which also contained a costly accompaniment of goldwork and jewellery. The story of this find, which lost nothing in the telling, soon reached the ears of the mudir of Qena who seized the coffin, had the mummy unwrapped in his harim and then took ship down the Nile to offer the treasure to Said as a personal gift. Mariette, learning of this act of piracy, and unwilling that the credit of his discoveries should be claimed by outsiders, set off in his official steam launch, intercepted the mudir's boat and succeeded by great effrontery and a show of force in recovering the treasure which he in turn presented to Said. Happily Said did not resent the manner in which his Conservator of Monuments had re-taken possession of the jewellery, nor did he claim it all for himself; but his Oriental mind was at last awakened to the importance and value of the antiquities that were being un-

Pls. 49–58

covered, and he gave orders that a museum worthy of housing such valuable finds should be established.[3]

The discovery of Ah-hotpe's jewels and trappings hardly ranks as serious archaeology since no reliable records were kept at the time of discovery, and some of the minor objects may have disappeared during the unwrapping in the mudir's harim. It is, for instance, impossible now to discover how the various elements in the unique

Pl. 55

Falcon Collar were strung originally, though such information was doubtless available at the moment of unwrapping.

Actually no large deposit of jewellery has been found intact by scientific excavation in Egypt apart from that recovered from the tomb of Tut-ankh-amun, and even there the personal jewels, as distinct from the funerary amulets, had mostly been stolen. De Morgan, excavating in 1894 and 1895 in the precincts of the ruined brick pyramids of Ammenemes II (*obit c.* 1895 BC) and Sesostris III (*obit. c.* 1843 BC) at Dahshur, had the good fortune to find the personal

Pls. 10–12, 27–31, 33, 34, 41, 42, 44–46

ornaments of six daughters of the royal house.[4] His methods of recovery, however, were defective and the crowns, pectorals, bracelets and necklaces were exhibited in their divorced parts for many years in the Cairo Museum until the study of the contemporary jewels from Lahun enabled them to be re-assembled into something approaching their original appearance and magnificence.

In 1914, Flinders Petrie, excavating the pyramid complex of Sesostris II (*obit. c.* 1878 BC) at Lahun, lighted upon the pit-tomb of Sit-Hathor-Yunet, a daughter of the king, who had been buried within the enclosure of her father's monument. Her burial had been rifled in antiquity and her body broken up to retrieve the funerary jewellery which adorned and protected it so ineffectually. But the robbers, working in frantic haste and by the feeble light of guttering lamps, had overlooked an obscure recess which housed her jewellery caskets, wig-chest and toilet boxes. These were subsequently covered with layers of mud washed into the chambers of the opened tomb by periodical floodings until the tomb-shaft was eventually choked with drifting sand. By the time Petrie's assistant, Guy

Brunton, came to clear the recess, it resembled a large dried-out mud pie into which various bits and pieces of the objects had been stirred by swirls of storm-water and debris. The decayed wood was little more than a brown stain in the circumambient mud and the corroded copper and silver were reduced to virtual green and purple smears. Brunton spent days and nights in the cramped conditions of the tomb, picking away at the mass of mud with a penknife and a pin, until he had recovered without damage the thousands of pieces both large and minute. He also managed to make a plan showing the position of each item as he came upon it during his slow clearance of the recess and his notes and diagrams proved of inestimable value when the reconstruction of the jewellery and casket was eventually undertaken.[5]

As the Lahun hoard seemed to duplicate the contemporary treasure from Dahshur, Petrie was allowed to keep the jewellery with the exception of Sit-Hathor-Yunet's mirror, crown and a pectoral, each of which was unique, and these remained in Cairo. Petrie subsequently sold the contents of the recess to the Metropolitan Museum in New York where two of the caskets were reconstructed with great skill and ingenuity by A. C. Mace and the original appearance of the jewellery was recovered by Herbert Winlock in a brilliant study of the entire deposit based upon Brunton's invaluable field work.[6] Only in two minor particulars did Winlock go astray, and Miss E. S. Eaton was subsequently able to show that the bird-claw necklace should be re-threaded to make two anklets.[7] William Hayes has also pointed out that the gold tubes on the great wig of Sit-Hathor-Yunet should be re-arranged in a chequer pattern.[8]

Pls. 38, 39

Pl. 152

Pls. 35–40

Pl. 36

Pl. 39

A similar deposit covered with water-laid mud and debris was found by Edward Ayrton in a pit-tomb (No. 56) in the Valley of the Kings at Thebes in 1908.[9] But it was excavated with far less skill and conscientiousness than Brunton had exercised at Lahun, and what was retrieved was for long regarded as part of the funerary equipment of Queen Twosre (*obit. c.* 1200 BC) hidden away by a robber or guardian in the pit in which it was found when her tomb (No. 14) was usurped by her successor Set-nakhte, and her burial evicted. There is little doubt, however, that what Ayrton found was the burial of an infant daughter of Twosre by her first husband, King Sethos II, and the child's meagre personal jewels had been supplemented with pieces from the queen's trinket boxes, including heirlooms.[10]

Pls. 130, 131

The discovery by Pierre Montet in 1939 of royal tombs of the Twenty-first and Twenty-second Dynasties at Tanis, has brought to light jewellery of the Late Period, mostly of a funerary character and maintaining the traditional design of such amuletic pectorals, collars and bracelets.[11] But it would appear that the burials of the Pharaohs in question had been disturbed and re-arranged in antiquity, and it is probable that their personal ornaments had long been filched by the time Montet came to uncover them. While in the mass the goldwork and jewels found at Tanis make an impressive show, it is clear that each king took to the tomb a far less opulent store of treasure than was buried with Tut-ankh-amun.

Pls. 135–140

In Egypt, as elsewhere, spectacular discoveries of such riches have more often been made by accident rather than as a result of deliberate search. Thus in 1906, while a railway embankment was being constructed at Zagazig in the Delta, near Tell Basta, the site of the ancient city of Bubastis, a hoard of gold and silver, mostly in the form of vessels but including bracelets of Ramesses II, was uncovered.[12] This was probably a cache hidden by a thief or temple official in troubled times and never reclaimed. The Antiquities Department had difficulty in establishing its right to all this treasure trove against the claims of a local dealer, and as a result some of the hoard is now in the Berlin and Metropolitan Museums. Such chance finds as that of the treasure of the queens of Tuthmosis III have usually been made by private persons who are only too willing to dispose of the objects to middlemen under a vow of secrecy; and it is seldom that such discoveries come to the ears of authority. In this way jewels have entered collections abroad with no details of the circumstances in which they were found, or at the best accompanied by a garbled and often deliberately misleading account. It is rare that the Cairo Museum has

Pl. 129

been able to take possession of such fortunate finds, a notable exception being the Tukh el-Qaramus hoard which was found by accident in 1905 when an ass, straying from the path, put its hoof through a large pot buried near the surface of the ground and revealed to its overjoyed rider the glitter of gold and silver that lay hidden within. Unfortunately for the finder he was seen to remove his prize to his home and nearly all its contents were recovered by the Antiquities Service before they could be dispersed.[13] They proved to be mostly of Hellenistic date and thus outside the scope of our survey.

Such treasure that has escaped the melting-pot during the last century and a half, whether it has been carefully uncovered by the archaeologist or by the hands of less scrupulous looters, now lies scattered among a hundred collections in Egypt, Europe and America. This fortuitous sampling of ancient jewellery, however, is unfortunately rather uneven. While we have representative examples from the Middle and New Kingdoms and are thus in a position to assess the achievement of these periods, the actual specimens of Old Kingdom date are very rare indeed and reflect mostly a funerary art. The Saite period, which was characterized by a return to the classic styles of earlier ages, expressed by meticulous and unfaltering techniques, is unrepresented except by a few battered funerary amulets. In the latest periods of Pharaonic history, the native jewellery is replaced by Persian and Hellenistic designs favoured by those of the ruling classes who could afford such an expensive luxury.

Despite the incomplete nature of this conspectus, Egyptian jewellery in the mass forms a most impressive testimony to the skill and taste of the ancient craftsman, making its appeal by its effective design and the glowing colours of each jewel considered as a whole. In this it bears a closer resemblance to medieval stained glass than it does to modern jewellery. Precious gemstones employed in the making of modern expensive jewels were unknown to the ancient Egyptians who selected their materials for their colour and polish rather than their refractive powers, brilliance and rarity.

CHAPTER TWO

The Uses of Ancient Egyptian Jewellery

It should be obvious from the foregoing chapter that what has survived today is but an infinitesimal proportion of the jewellery that was produced in Egypt during the three millennia of its history under the Pharaohs. In the first place, personal adornments were worn in life by men as well as women and these were not restricted to fingerrings but could include bracelets, anklets, collars, necklaces and, at some periods, even ear-rings and fillets. Everyone who could afford a burial, however modest, expected to be tricked out in his finery after death and even the poorest inhumations do not lack a string or two of beads around the neck or arm of the deceased. The sands of the necropolis at Saqqara are so rich with the 'mummy beads' of disturbed burials that the stringing of them as necklaces for sale to tourists is a venerable local industry.

The gods, too, had their jewellery. Every shrine sheltered the statue or statues of gods which had to have a change of raiment, including jewellery and especially collars, as part of the daily ritual of service. The temple magazines held impressive quantities of jewels, as we can read from their inventories, though of course all have long since been looted and only a miserable huddle of discarded treasure found hidden in the precincts of the temple of Dendera[1] bears any witness to the wealth that was once stored in temple repositories. The pictures of the furnishings provided by Tuthmosis III for the temple of Amun at Karnak, and shown sculptured on the south wall of a chamber adjacent to the sanctuary, include a catalogue of the various gold necklaces, collars and bracelets which he supplied for the service of the god. With such widespread patronage it is clear that the occupation of jeweller must have been one of the most flourishing in ancient Egypt throughout its long history.

cf. Pl. 146

Pl. 119

Jewels, by which we mean any ornament designed to adorn the person, may be worn for various reasons, but probably their fundamental and most compelling purpose in ancient Egypt was as amulets for the protection of the wearer from mysterious hostile forces. These might manifest themselves in tangible forms such as noxious animals, crocodiles, snakes, scorpions and the like; or they might take a less visible shape and appear as disease, accidents and such natural calamities as flood, storm and drought. To protect himself against such inimical powers, the ancient primitive, like his modern counterpart, tied charms to his wrists, ankles, neck, waist and other vulnerable points. Such talismans might consist of various stones, such as the carnelian, turquoise and lapis lazuli, that preserved within themselves the colour of life-blood, the fresh green of springing vegetation or the blue of water and the holy sky-realms. The pebbles had to be perforated before they could be attached by linen cords or leather thongs; thus the stone pendant was introduced and later supplemented by various shaped beads in such artificial materials as pottery, green or blue glazed steatite, glazed quartz frit ('faience') and glass.

Among such magic substances must also be included gold, which was probably first found as shining granules in river sands. Gold could be worked by comparatively simple means and fashioned into gleaming beads and objects that never lost their lustre but seemed to retain within themselves all the fire and glory of the sun. No wonder, therefore, that the flesh of the very gods was believed to be made of this eternally shining material.

The claws of birds of prey and other ferocious creatures, or the horns and tusks of wild animals were also thought to contain magic virtues that could be turned to the advantage of the possessor of such *disjecta membra*; and prehistoric amulets often take these forms though only the bird claws survived as the amulets of historic times, and even they are not found after the Middle Kingdom.

Pls. 12, 36

Another natural product that aroused primitive wonder was the shell of fresh and sea water animals. Bracelets could be ground out of the conus shell. The cowrie shell with its indented lip has the appear-

Pls. 2, 29, 45

1 *Wedjet* eye

2 *Sa*-sign

3 *Ankh*-sign

4 *Tyet*-sign

Pl. 33

Pls. 106, 108

Pl. 12

Pl. 30

Pls. 31, 44

Pls. 104, 107

Pl. 5

ance of a half-closed but ever watching eye and was therefore thought to be, by sympathetic means, a prophylactic against the evil eye, a belief in the blasting powers of which is still widespread around the shores of the Mediterranean and in East Africa. Even in recent times Nilotic women have worn aprons sewn with cowrie shells to protect the pelvic organs from the aborting and sterilizing effect of a malevolent gaze. The cowrie shell and the cowroid design were used in ancient Egypt for the same purpose though in time they were supplemented and replaced by the *wedjet* eye of the sky-god Horus which, with the scarab, is probably the commonest amulet found in ancient Egypt.

The 'Eye of Horus' was but one of a whole host of symbols that came into existence with the invention of hieroglyphic writing and could have significance as protective devices. Thus an object fashioned as the *sa*-sign, a rolled-up papyrus shelter with the meaning 'protection', could be used as a general defence against any hostile force. Moreover, other symbols could play a more positive role, and the *ankh* (a sandal strap) or the *tyet* (a girdle tie) or the *djed* (a column of trimmed papyrus stalks) could promise their bearer 'life', 'welfare', 'endurance' and the like. Small images of the gods, or their familiar animals, could place the wearer under the direct protection of the deity. Lastly amulets in the form of glyphs could be combined into brief mottoes or expressions of good wishes, or the names of kings regarded as protective deities. Such compositions are particularly characteristic of the Middle Kingdom jewels from Dahshur and Lahun; but many of the jewels from the tomb of Tut-ankh-amun are also designed upon elements forming the name of the king.

The amuletic character of Egyptian jewellery underlies most of its forms and purposes, particularly in the case of that made to be placed upon the peculiarly vulnerable mummy of the deceased. Such funerary charms are often of a flimsy construction, consisting of thin layers of metal foil upon a plaster filling and having cheap substitutes for hard stone inlays or beads, since it was not called upon to suffer the abrasive wear of everyday life. Funerary jewellery, in fact, follows traditional designs which vary little from one age to the next, and which have been tabulated and often captioned in the pictures painted on the insides of wooden coffins in the First Intermediate Period and Middle Kingdom, as substitutes for the real things or as supplements of them.

Figs. 23–27

Jewels could also be used as an extension of their magic powers to enhance the sexual attractiveness of the wearer, in the same way as dress and cosmetics were employed. It is when the adornment of the person becomes paramount that the artistic aspects of the jewel become as important as its amuletic significance. Thus fillets and circlets were devised more to keep the hair in a pleasing shape than to protect the head. The artificial cowrie shells in the girdle around the waist could be filled with rattling pellets to give forth a seductive tinkle as the wearer swayed her hips in walking. Cunningly designed anklets and bracelets could enhance a slender limb or disguise a thickened joint.

Pl. 35

5 *Djed*-sign

For such aids to beauty, wreaths, chaplets and collars of fresh flowers were an inevitable choice; and the industry of the florist must have been among the earliest and longest-lived in Egypt. A lotus bud was usually tucked in the hair of guests at feasts. Collars made by sewing flower-petals, leaves, fruits and seeds onto semi-circular or penannular sheets of papyrus or strips of palm leaf were supplied as ephemeral decorations. Even the boatmen in the marshlands would take a handful of dripping water-weed with all its twined flowers and weave it into a chaplet to keep the hair in place against the gusts of the strong north wind. On gala days they might stick lotus blooms into such fillets and hang wreaths of the freshly plucked flowers from their necks.

Pl. 67

6 Herdsman from a painting in the tomb of Itet at Meydum

The jewellers early contrived to translate into less transitory materials the colour and design of such natural forms, and their creations underwent a constant development. Perhaps the two crowns from Dahshur, one a naturalistic transformation and the other a more stylized interpretation of the floral archetype, are among their outstanding triumphs in this field. It is perhaps not with-

Pls. 27, 28

out significance that the generic Egyptian word for 'jewellery' appears to refer to imitation plants and flowers.[2]

As elsewhere, jewels could also be used to exhibit the status and wealth, and therefore the power and prestige, of the owner. In *The Lamentations of Ipuwer,* the sage, in describing the effects of political decay and social revolution during the twilight of the Middle Kingdom[3] which have turned his world topsy-turvy, bewails that 'gold and lapis lazuli, silver and turquoise, carnelian (?) and amethyst are hung around the necks of slave girls while noble ladies walk through the land and house-mistresses are forced to beg.'[4] Rich jewels in ancient Egypt could not be displayed on any scale of magnificence except as the rewards of the king: and it is clear that, as in modern Europe, one of the responsibilities of the Court jewellers was the making of valuable orders and decorations for bestowal by the Pharaoh upon favoured officials.

The Order of the Golden Collar was perhaps the oldest of such honours, and one of the treasure chambers of Sahure's funerary temple has provided us with an early record (*c.* 2475 BC) of the investiture by the king of his courtiers with collars, diadems and seals under the general description of 'The Award of Gold.'[5] Sabni, one of the border barons of Elephantine, boasts how he was summoned to the Residence in Memphis and there decorated with 'the gold of favour' by Phiops II for leading successful missions into Nubia and the Sudan (*c.* 2200 BC).[6] It also seems to have been the practice for the great feudal lords during the Old Kingdom to ape their king in rewarding followers with gold ornaments. Thus Neb-em-akhet, a son of King Mykerinos of the Fourth Dynasty, presents gold necklaces to dancers who entertain him on a relief in his tomb.[7] In the New Kingdom, the 'gold of honour' had taken a different form and strings of gold disk beads *(shebyu)* were hung around the necks of the persons whom the king wished to honour on special state occasions. In some representations the recipient is shown bowed down under a number of such necklaces. Even in the fourth century BC a so-called Neo-Memphite relief in Cairo shows the award of gold collars of the

Pls. 48, 117

Pl. 120

Pl. 149

earlier type; and it would be rash to claim that this is a purely fictitious scene harking back, in the archaistic manner of such reliefs, to an event which existed only in the past.

Another mark of rank was the Order of the Golden Fly, which first makes its appearance during the early New Kingdom under increased influence from Asia. This award, which appears to be of military significance, was given particularly for valour, and the soldier Ah-mose-pen-Nekheb, who fought under the early kings of the Eighteenth Dynasty, boasts that he received no less than six flies from Tuthmosis I.[8] The order could apparently also be given to women, for Queen Ah-hotpe, who rallied the Theban forces at a critical moment in the struggle against the Hyksos hegemony, had three large boldly designed flies among her treasure.[9] One at least Pl. 53 of the queens of Tuthmosis III was buried with a necklace of small flies also in gold. Gold lions and bracelets were included in such re- Pl. 86 wards,[10] which together with other valuable objects in precious metals, such as parade weapons, took the place of money in an age when coinage still remained to be invented.

Such jewels were the work of craftsmen attached to the Court and were generally distributed by the king, particularly on such ceremonial occasions as his coronation and jubilees. In the tomb of Kheruef at Thebes, for instance, there is a scene showing Amenophis III presiding at the distribution to his officials of decorations or re- wards in the form of gold fishes, birds and plants during his First Jubilee. The king, as the wealthiest and most active of patrons, would give constant employment to his goldsmiths and jewellers. They had to prepare complete parures not only for himself on his accession but also for his wives on their marriage to him, unless they were the daughters of foreign potentates, in which case their personal ornaments were evidently supplied by their fathers as part of their dowry.[11] Nevertheless the three Syrian wives of Tuthmosis III had only one or two items of un-Egyptian design and nearly all their jewels bear the name of their husband who must have provided them. Gifts in the form of jewels, particularly of gold, were sent with des-

7 Pectoral of Surero

8 Pectorals of Kheruef

Pls. 87–89

9 Huy receiving
Tut-ankh-amun's
signet

patches to foreign potentates who sometimes commissioned work from Egyptian craftsmen.[12]

The funerary jewels of the king and his relations would also have to be prepared as part of his burial equipment from the first years of his reign, and these would be of a more traditional and less individual design than the ornaments worn in everyday life. At the king's jubilees it would appear that new jewels were made; and both Surero and Kheruef are shown presenting pectorals to Amenophis III on the occasion of that monarch's Jubilees. We are also fortunate in having several of the carved gems made for insertion in gold bracelets for this same celebration. One specimen shows the diminutive figure of the donor, a high official, holding his fan of office behind Queen Tiye, and gives evidence that on such great occasions valuable gifts were offered to the Royal Family by their courtiers, either from their bounty or by virtue of the duties of their office.[13]

Lastly, jewels could be made for purely utilitarian reasons. Massive cylinder seals of gold or hardstone mounted in gold and bearing the king's name were conferred on those high officials who were to act in the name of the Pharaoh during the Old and Middle Kingdoms.[14] In the New Kingdom the seal was replaced by a heavy signet ring, the bezel of which bore the king's cartouche. Probably also to be included in this category of objects of utility are the *menyet* necklaces and counterpoises that were carried by great ladies or priestesses as symbols of their devotion to the cult of the goddess Hathor or her avatars.

1 Bracelets from the tomb of King Djer, from Abydos ▷

2 Gold ornaments of the Archaic Period, from Nag-ed-Der ▷

6 Gold wig ornaments and fillet of Seneb-tisi, from Lisht ▷

3 Silver inlaid bracelets of Queen Hetep-her-es, from Giza

4 Gold fillet of a princess, from Giza

5 Gold beetle necklace of a princess, from Giza

7 Gold, stone and faience Falcon Collar of Seneb-tisi, from Lisht

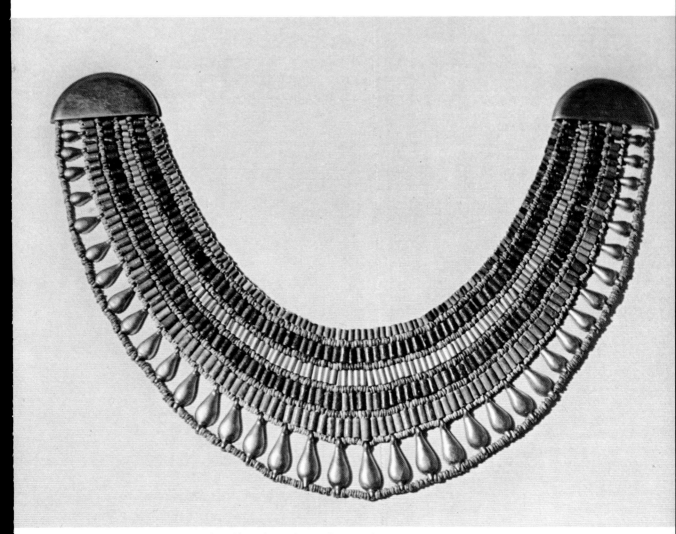

8 Gold, stone and faience Broad Collar of Seneb-tisi, from Lisht

9 Bead belt and apron of Seneb-tisi, from Lisht

10 Broad Collar, counterpoise and bracelet of Princess Ita-weret, from Dahshur

11 Falcon Collar of Princess Khnumet, from Dahshur

12 Funerary jewels of Princess Khnumet, from Dahshur

CHAPTER THREE

The Materials

Gold was the ineluctable material from which Egyptian jewellery came to be fashioned. Modern precious metals such as platinum, rhodium, and palladium were virtually unknown to the ancient world, but their shining white appearance could be achieved by various alloys of silver and gold occurring in the natural state. The qualities that made gold so desirable have already been enumerated. It could be won and worked with comparative ease: it did not decay or tarnish in use but was indestructible, and its warm colour seemed to reflect the fire and brilliance of the sun. Egypt was fortunate in having within its boundaries immense deposits of gold, the richest by far of the ancient world. Modern experts, investigating the skill and diligence with which the ancient gold-fields were exploited, have reported that the Egyptians were very thorough prospectors and miners. No workable deposits have yet been discovered that they overlooked.[1] It seems clear that by the Nineteenth Dynasty they had exhausted the more accessible supplies, for both Sethos I and Ramesses II had to open up mines deeper in the Eastern Desert, where wells supplying subterranean water required for the washing of the crushed ore and the sustenance of the workers could not easily be found.[2] A map on a damaged sheet of papyrus from this period shows *Fig. 10* some mines, probably in the Wady Hammamat.

Much of the gold, and certainly that which was won in earliest times, was found in metallic form as shining granules among sands and gravels. Its collection and melting into larger rings or ingots were not difficult processes and well within the ability of primitive peoples. It is possible that much of the gold levied in the New Kingdom as an annual tax upon Nubia and the Lower Sudan, as well as upon certain towns in Upper Egypt such as Koptos, Edfu, Esna and Hierakonpolis which had connections with the Eastern Desert, was

10   Map of the gold mines in the Wady Hammamat

collected in this way. It is shown in tribute scenes either as ring-shaped ingots or as gold dust contained in red leather bags.[3] Minimum amounts appear to have been fixed every year and such metal entered into the state magazines, whether of the king or of the larger temples. It is also probable that a certain amount of gold won by the same processes found its way by private trading into the free market to be used for the jewels of those citizens who could afford such luxuries.

Later and more advanced methods of mining involved the extraction of gold from veins in quartz rock, which had to be fractured by quenching areas previously heated by fire, pounding and grinding the broken portions, and panning the powder to separate the heavier metal particles. Such work was very laborious and performed, at least in Ptolemaic and Roman times, by criminals.[4] Earlier the army, which was often used as a labour force, may have been employed on such work as well as captives.[5]

Egyptian gold contains impurities mostly in the form of silver, which, when it amounts to as much as a fifth of the whole, becomes the pale amber-coloured alloy, electrum (Greek: *electron*). A higher proportion of silver produces a white metal indistinguishable in appearance from silver. Egyptian gold also contains varying percentages of other metals, chiefly copper, iron and sometimes platinum.[6] It is clear that in remote antiquity goldsmiths must have relied upon colour and surface appearance for their assays, since they speak in one place of 'green gold' by which they presumably mean gold containing a fair proportion of silver.[7] The Amarna Letters show that gold was tested by casting it into a furnace whence it did not always emerge weighing as much as it did before.[8] This would suggest that, by the New Kingdom at the latest, the refining of gold was understood and carried out presumably by the cupellation process.[9] Since at this period the smelting of bronze from copper and tin ores was widely practised, it is probable that improved metallurgical skills led to the discovery that alloys of gold such as electrum could be artificially produced. By the end of the Eighteenth Dynasty the Egyptians had certainly learnt to make an alloy of copper and gold which would hardly appear in nature,[10] and it is reasonable to suggest that similar experiments were conducted with other metals. As a result of the passage of time much ancient gold-work has acquired a grey, reddish brown or plum-purple patina due to the tarnishing of the copper, iron and silver components. It is evident, for instance, that in some of the jewels of Tut-ankh-amun gold was selected which has radically changed its colour over the centuries, very probably as the result of the deliberate introduction of other metals to alloy with it. This explains why the Babylonian rulers

Pl. 69

Pls. 95, 96

were not averse to casting into the furnace the gold they received from Egypt to see whether it was as pure as it pretended to be.

Some goldwork during the New Kingdom from the Amarna Period until the end of the Ramessids (i.e. from 1370 to 1080 BC) has a shining rose-purple patination, which so far from being the result of slow chemical change over the centuries is an intentional effect apparently achieved by introducing iron salts into the metal at some stage of manufacture.[11] It has been plausibly suggested that the addition of 'fool's gold' (iron pyrites) to the metal while it was being melted may very well have achieved this distinctive colouration which is due to a very fine film of iron oxide on the surface of the gold.[12] Such coloured goldwork or the secrets of its manufacture evidently came from Asia, for one of the Amarna Letters from the King of Mitanni, listing the gifts that he was sending to Amenophis III, speaks of ornaments of gold 'through which blood shines.'[13] The Egyptian name for this coloured gold is unknown. Some specimens, such as the openwork ornaments of Tut-ankh-amun, show both the pink colour of the treated metal and the yellow gleam of the natural gold, but this could easily have been achieved by scraping away the extremely fine film of oxide in selected areas.[14]

Cf. Pls. 122, 131, 134

Electrum was a naturally occuring alloy of gold and silver imported from the Eastern Desert and from the land of Punt, believed to have lain somewhere on the Somali coast. The evidence suggests that in earliest times its relationship to gold was not properly understood and it was classified as a separate metal.[15] By the New Kingdom, however, it is almost certain that it was being produced artificially.

Silver to the ancient Egyptian was another form of gold, for he called it 'white gold', which should not be confused with its modern counterpart made from gold alloyed with nickel or platinum. In this, the ancient Egyptian seems to have spoken truer than he knew, for nearly all the silver found in the Old and Middle Kingdoms has a high proportion of gold in its composition varying from as much as 38 per cent down to 9.[16] The name given to the metal by the Egyptians suggests that it was found in association with gold and it is in fact a low grade of gold containing so much silver as to be grey-white in colour. The metallurgical techniques required to smelt silver from its ores were probably not within the knowledge of the Egyptians at this period, and most Egyptian silver shows specks of gold unevenly distributed over its surface. The discovery that silver could be obtained from smelting argentiferous lead ores appears to have been made in Western Asia whence it began to be imported, particularly from the time of the New Kingdom onwards, though the Treasure of Tod, a deposit mostly of silver objects and ingots contained in four boxes bearing the names of Ammenemes II (*obit c.* 1895 BC) and buried under the foundations of a Middle Kingdom temple, bears strong evidence that it derives from an, as yet unknown, Asiatic source.[17]

Silver was rarer than gold in Egypt and was probably for that reason more highly prized until the Middle Kingdom, when imports from Asia began to arrive. The bracelets of Queen Hetep-her-es   Pl. 3 of the Fourth Dynasty, though massive in appearance, are actually thin shells of silver, whereas the gold on her furniture was lavishly applied. Even at the time of Tut-ankh-amun little silver was used in his funerary equipment, the only sizable pieces being one of the trumpets and a vessel in the form of a pomegranate, though at least three silver jugs and a seal on a chain had been stolen from it, according to a label listing the contents of a broken box.[18] The amount of silver buried on ancient Egyptian sites, however, was originally far greater than what has been recovered because, apart from losses due to plundering, silver unlike gold corrodes in contact with salt-impregnated soils, and cannot be restored if mineralization is complete.

Gold, electrum, and to a lesser extent silver were the noble metals used for setting the gemstones which we would now classify as no more than semi-precious. The Egyptian chose them for their rich colours, not their refractive powers, and the classic trio that formed the basis of his colour schemes for jewellery were the blood-red carnelian, the vivid blue-green of turquoise and the deep cerulean blue lapis lazuli. The lust to possess such stones sent Egyptian prospectors into the Eastern Desert, where carnelian pebbles could be picked up without much difficulty, and into Sinai where turquoise had to be mined laboriously from veins in sandstone outcrops. Lapis lazuli, however, was not found within the borders of Egypt and had to be imported from the Euphrates area whither it had been traded from Badakhshan in Afghanistan. It has been suggested that the Egyptian name for the stone, *khesbed,* is a variant of this toponym.[19] These hardstones were not only used for inlays but also for beads in which form they are known from the predynastic period, an indication of the extreme antiquity of trade routes.

A list of craftsmen in a papyrus in the British Museum[20] mentions a *mes'at* or 'purveyor of precious stones', who may have been a sort of prospector roving the desert and collecting its produce, whether animal or vegetable besides mineral. In addition to carnelian, other red stones capable of taking a high polish were sought out, such as red jasper and garnets which often occur in nature in the form of dodecahedral crystals; it requires very little working to turn them into beads. Often the garnets are shed from their matrix by weathering and form beaches of spheroidal stones which need only to be perforated to become beads. Egyptian garnets which are found at Aswan tend to be too small for use, but larger specimens came from Western Sinai.[21] The popularity of garnets in the Middle Kingdom may be due to the intensive exploitation of minerals in Sinai during that period.

Cf. Pl. 43   An alternative stone used in place of turquoise is green felspar, the Amazon Stone, of an opaque rich green tint, which is sometimes distinctly blue, and is easily broken along its two dominant planes of cleavage. A broad seam of the stone with evidences of ancient working has been found in the Eastern Desert.[22] It was used for beads, particularly during the Middle Kingdom, and was still being employed for amulets and inlays during the time of Tut-ankh-amun.

Amethyst, which occurs in cavities in granite rocks, was used exclusively for beads and pendants, and occasionally for scarabs,
Pl. 109   even as late as the reign of Tut-ankh-amun. Though its popularity

was greatest at the time of the Middle Kingdom, it appears as early as the First Dynasty in one of the bracelets of King Djer (*c.* 3000 BC). It is, however, a stone of a colour that has to be used with discretion and it says much for the restraint of the Egyptian jeweller that he refrained from employing it as an inlay. Ancient amethyst workings have been found in the Aswan district, the Eastern Desert, and in the region of Abu Simbel.[23] The rhomboidal crystals of the stone can be weathered or ground into ovoid or spheroid shapes, which were most commonly worked into beads.

Other stones used sporadically in Pharaonic times were yellow, green and brown jaspers, rock crystal, obsidian, banded chalcedony and calcite. The beryl is found only in jewellery of Hellenistic date.

From earliest times the Egyptians tried to find natural and artificial substitutes for their classical gemstones. By the time of Tut-ankhamun they were using Iceland spar, a pure and transparent form of calcite, and rock-crystal, both backed by coloured cements as inlays.[24] But their greatest need was for a dark blue substance which imitated the expensive imported lapis lazuli, and their search for such a substitute was pursued with all the diligence that European chemists in the eighteenth century exercised in their endeavours to imitate Chinese porcelain. In predynastic times they had discovered not only how to coat soapstone with an alkaline blue or green glaze but also how to fire powdered quartz into a compact substance covered with a gleaming vitreous glaze coloured green and blue from copper compounds. Later they developed black, red, white, yellow, and lilac glazes on the same body. Such materials could be easily carved or moulded into beads of various shapes and sizes.

In certain circumstances, with a greater proportion of alkali and rather higher temperatures, small quantities of the ingredients used in faience-making will fuse into a bright blue or green frit which, when ground up, can be used as a glazing substance or as a pigment. By the Fourth Dynasty at the latest, the Egyptians had succeeded in making a crystalline lapis blue material which owes its colour to the presence of copper calcium tetrasilicate.[25] This substance, generally

Pl. 1

Cf. Pls. 94, 95, 99, 100

Pls. 38, 40, 64

known as 'Egyptian blue', the *coeruleum* of Pliny, was exported to Rome in Imperial times where it was used as the standard blue pigment for wall-paintings, and only disappeared finally from the artist's palette in the seventh century AD. It is probable that the blue inlays used in some of the jewellery from Lahun and western Thebes were of this substance, though they had changed to a whitish powder in the damp mud that eventually buried them.

Frit is a form of glass, and isolated examples of glass as beads are found from the Fifth Dynasty to the beginning of the New Kingdom, the most notable example perhaps being the string containing small bright blue glass specimens together with silver, carnelian and green felspar found on the neck of an infant of the family of King Mentuhotpe II (*c.* 2050 BC).[26] The introduction of glass on an ambitious scale as an intentionally made material occurs only in the New Kingdom, the earliest datable pieces bearing the name of Tuthmosis III. The royal patronage of the new craft is seen in the proximity of glass factories to the palaces at Thebes, Amarna and Ghurab. It is probable that the making of glass in any quantity had to await the invention of the bellows-operated blast furnace, and increased interest and experimentation in the fusion of different ores which must have marked the introduction of bronze on a wide scale in Egypt during the New Kingdom, when copper was displaced as the metal in general use.[27] From the fact that the blue colour of Egyptian glass often comes from cobalt compounds which are not found in Egypt, it has been deduced that glass was not an Egyptian invention despite its occasional and accidental emergence as a by-product of the making of faience.[28]

Ancient Egyptian glass is a soda-lime silicate, not dissimilar in composition to modern glass, but containing a lower proportion of silica and lime. It was, however, usually opaque, though it is sometimes translucent and even occasionally transparent. Its main quality, when it is found in a good state of preservation, is the brilliance and intensity of its colours, yellow, white, black, red, green, dark blue, light blue and greenish blue. The Egyptian found that in glass he could produce a number of close imitations of his classic gemstones,

13 Gold bracelet of King Kha-sekhem-wy,
    from Abydos

14 Gold bracelet
    of King Sekhem-khet,
    from Saqqara

15 Limestone relief
    of Prince Khufu-khaf and
    his wife in his tomb at Giza

16 Plaster and copper 'boatman's circlet', from Giza

17 Relief of boatmen fighting, mastaba of Ptah-sekhem-ankh, from Saqqara

19 Gold and faience Broad Collar of Impy

20 Faience Broad Collar of Wah, from Thebes

21 Inscribed silver scarab of Wah, from Thebes

22 Necklaces of Wah, from Thebes

23 Relief of dancing-girls with hair ornaments,
from the tomb of Queen Nofru at Thebes

24 Seated statue of Queen Nofret, from Tanis ▷

25, 26 Front and rear views of a Middle Kingdom pectoral

and he used them in his jewellery with enthusiasm, as so many of the furnishings from the tomb of Tut-ankh-amun bear witness. That the Egyptian was deliberately trying to imitate stones as much as creating a new substance is seen in his description of glass as 'melted stones'.[29] Lest it be thought that 'glass' with its modern connotation suggests a rather cheap and inferior product, it must be emphasized that Egyptian glass, despite its brilliant colours, lacks a sparkling surface, and the minute bubbles of captive air give a texture to the substance which often makes it difficult to distinguish from that of the stone it is trying to imitate. Some of the objects from the tomb of Tut-ankh-amun have, for instance, been catalogued as inlaid with lapis lazuli, carnelian and felspar, when glass simulating those stones would have been a more accurate description.

Cf. Pl. 103

It is evident that the materials for Egyptian jewellery came almost exclusively from minerals mined or picked up in the Eastern Desert or Sinai. The early prospectors had no scientific means of distinguishing between various substances except by colour and hardness, and for this reason they included gold and silver in the same category as their precious stones, though they gave precedence to the former. On the other hand, naturally occurring gem stones are followed in the offering lists by the base metals, and they in turn by the artificial stones,[30] suggesting that the Egyptians realized that the last two classes of substance could both be made by smelting various ingredients which were very different from the resulting products.

It also suggests that the Egyptians regarded man-made products as inferior to those that the gods had provided. The chief deity of the deserts, from which all the beautiful materials of jewellery came, was Hathor, the goddess of love and beauty. She was particularly associated with jewellery and it is perhaps significant that her priestesses carried an elaborate *menyet* necklace as a symbol of her cult. She was also the patron of miners and prospectors who roved over the region and exploited its minerals.

11 Priestess of Hathor with a *menyet*

Pl. 114

CHAPTER FOUR

The Craftsmen and their Tools

In the so-called *Satire on the Trades,* which the Egyptian schoolboy was expected to copy as part of his onerous training, and in order to encourage his flagging resolution, the privileged lot of the scribe is contrasted with that of less favoured workers. 'I have never seen a goldsmith sent [on an important mission]', declares the author, 'but I have seen the metal-worker at the mouth of his brazier. His fingers were dried and wrinkled like the skin of a crocodile, and he stank worse than the roe of fishes.'[1] Such lampoons tend to obscure the esteem that was felt for the craftsmen who produced jewels in such abundance for their wealthy clients. Apuia, one of the chief goldsmiths of Amenophis III, was influential enough to build a handsome tomb for himself in the necropolis of Memphis;[2] and his son, Pa-ren-nefer, who held a like office under Akhenaten, not only had a large sculptured tomb at Thebes, but an equally important one at Amarna also.[3] Pa-ren-nefer, in fact, was sufficiently intimate with the king to be appointed his cup-bearer.

Fig. 12   It may well be that the apprentices and journeymen who actually sat over the heat of their charcoal braziers manipulating their blow-pipes and tongs were inferior in the social scale to the artists who designed the jewels and supervised their manufacture, but they were certainly not unprivileged. The favoured position and modest affluence enjoyed by the mortuary craftsmen of Deir el-Medina suggest that all similar adepts at highly regarded trades could command the respect and purses of their patrons.

The gold deposits in the deserts bordering Egypt and Nubia were the most considerable of the ancient world and it is probable that the techniques of extracting the metal and its alloys and working it were largely Egyptian discoveries. Such knowledge would have

12   Man at a brazier

been handed down over the centuries from father to son as a closely guarded mystique; and while there is no evidence for the existence of guilds of goldsmiths it is probable that the craft of the jeweller remained in the hands of a limited number of families working in one or two favoured localities. It is to be suspected, for instance, that the ancient northern capital Memphis, with the artificer Ptah as its patron deity, housed the most important goldsmiths' quarter, a tradition which persisted in medieval times and survived until recently in the metal-workers of the Cairo bazaars. It is also not improbable that accomplished workmen from other areas of the Mediterranean may have been attracted to this centre, drawn by the demand for jewellery, and the opportunities for patronage at a period of high culture and prosperity. As gold was a precious material, and its control and use the chief interest of kings, goldsmiths were a privileged community who worked mostly in royal workshops, or those attached to cults under royal protection. If their patrons withdrew their support for any reason, such as anarchy, conquest or impoverishment, the goldsmiths could migrate to wherever their luxurious trade was welcome. By the New Kingdom it would seem that the goldsmith's techniques were practically universal over the Near East, and it is sometimes difficult to claim certain goldwork found in Egypt as exclusively native in design and manufacture.[4]   Pls. 55, 59

Besides the king, such wealthy patrons as the gods of the larger cities, particularly Amun of Thebes, employed goldsmiths in their workshops. Three overseers of goldsmiths were rich enough to have tombs in the Theban necropolis,[5] while the exact location of five others has been lost.[6] In addition it is known that two other goldsmiths, perhaps connected with the Court, had tombs at Thebes.[7] A number of relatively expensive monuments made for goldworkers are scattered among the world's collections.[8] Such men were doubtless highly skilled craftsmen, but they were not necessarily the designers of the jewels that they were called upon to make, apart from those of traditional pattern which varied little from one generation to the next. The designs of Court jewels would have to be changed, in some particulars at least, with each reign; and original artists might very well have added striking novelties to the old stock of patterns. The Dahshur and Lahun jewels show how changes could be rung on familiar themes. All the pectorals differ in their designs with the exception of one belonging to the Princess Sit-Hathor-Yunet, which appears to be a copy of an earlier model, and made by an uninspired workman.

Cf. Pls. 37, 38

The chief jewellers were doubtless literate men who had had the general training of a scribe but had specialized in the decorative arts. They probably knew all the techniques used by the goldsmiths and lapidaries though they may not necessarily have been proficient in them. The chief sculptor Neb-Amun, who lived under Amenophis III and was evidently a designer who could produce the drawings and cartoons for all objects of applied art besides sculpture, is shown in the paintings in his tomb examining the products of metal workers, joiners and other craftsmen, which are brought to him for his inspection and approval.[9] The Second Prophets of Amun at Thebes during the New Kingdom seem to have had special responsibilities for supervising various constructions and commissions on behalf of their king as well as their god. Thus paintings in the tombs of some of these officials show them examining the work of several craftsmen in the workshops attached to the temple of Amun, including the goldsmiths' ateliers where the weighing-out of the gold and silver to be allocated to the various jobs is done under the eye of one of their officers.[10] The rich funerary equipment, embellished with gold and silver and inlaid with semi-precious stones and coloured glass, which Amenophis III provided for his parents-in-law, was made under the supervision of their son, the Second Prophet of Amun, though unfortunately the valuable jewels that must have been supplied as part of the gift had been stolen by the time the tomb was discovered in 1905.[11] There is even some evidence that Tuthmosis III may not have disdained to design a set of vessels for the treasure he dedicated to the temple at Karnak. Certainly the chief sculptor of Akhenaten confesses that the king himself instructed him.[12] This probably

Pl. 148

Pl. 119

27 Crown of Princess Khnumet, from Dahshur ▷

28 Floral circlet of Princess Khnumet, from Dahshur ▷

29 Granular jewellery of Princess Khnumet, from Dahshur

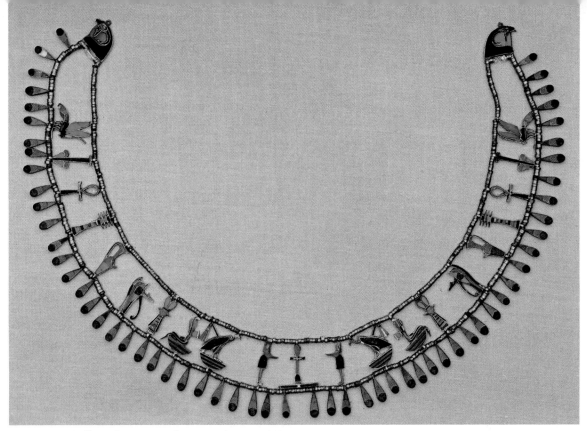

30 Falcon Collar of Princess Khnumet, from Dahshur

31 Motto clasps of Princess Khnumet, from Dahshur

33 Pectoral and necklace of Princess Sit-Hathor, from Dahshur

◁ 32 Wall-painting of the daughters of Djehuti-hotpe,
from his tomb at Deir el-Bersha

34 Jewellery of Princess Sit-Hathor, from Dahshur

35 Gold cowrie-shell girdle of Princess Sit-Hathor-Yunet, from Lahun

36 Gold leopard-head girdle and claw anklets of Princess Sit-Hathor-Yunet, from Lahun

37 First pectoral of Princess Sit-Hathor-Yunet, from Lahun

38 Second pectoral of Princess Sit-Hathor-Yunet, from Lahun

39 Wig ornaments and crown of Princess Sit-Hathor-Yunet, from Lahun ▷

40 Bead bracelet of Princess Sit-Hathor-Yunet, from Lahun

41 First pectoral of Queen Mereret, from Dahshur

42 Second pectoral of Queen Mereret, from Dahshur

43 Uraeus of Sesostris II, from Lahun

44 Jewellery of Queen Mereret, from Dahshur

45 Girdle and shell pectorals of Queen Mereret, from Dahshur

46 Jewellery of Queen Mereret, from Dahshur

47 Bead necklaces of the Middle Kingdom

48 Gold *shebyu* collar and parure, from Qurna

49   Bead bracelets of Queen Ah-hotpe, from Western Thebes

50   Pectoral of Queen Ah-hotpe, from Western Thebes

51   Armlet of Queen Ah-hotpe with sphinxes, from Western Thebes

52   Armlet of Queen Ah-hotpe with sphinxes, from Western Thebes

13 Goldsmiths at work

means that Akhenaten also stipulated the design of the jewels which he presented so lavishly to his family and friends. Pl. 118

In the Old Kingdom, it would appear that the chief priests of the artificer god Ptah of Memphis, who bore the title of 'Greatest of Craftsmen', were responsible for the designing of works of art both great and small, including jewellery. In reliefs of this period, dwarfs Fig. 13 are frequently shown handling the finished ornaments. In view of the fact that Ptah can appear in the form of the dwarf Patek, such dwarfs may have had some connection with the making of jewellery; but it is more likely that, as they were chiefly employed as valets and personal attendants upon the Royal Family and high Court officials, they were more concerned with assembling and storing such adjuncts of clothing in their masters' wardrobes.

The jewellers *par excellence* were, of course, the gold and silver-smiths, as is the case even today, but a list of craftsmen in the Hood Papyrus already referred to,[13] shows that there were minor specialists among this group of workers. Thus the *nuby*, or goldsmith, is immediately followed by the *neshdy,* or worker in precious stones, whom today we would call a lapidary since his products were suitable for inlaying in wooden and stone furniture besides metal settings.

There was also a *baba*, or faience-maker, a firer of glaze, who practised the art of firing a quartz paste into moulded shapes generally with a brilliant blue or green glassy surface, but later in other colours as well, or combinations of two or more colours in the same piece. In the New Kingdom he doubtless added the new-fangled art of making glass to his repertoire of skills. Another member of the jewellers' fraternity was the *setro* who appears to have been a maker of necklaces, a skilled occupation as anyone will know who has attempted to reconstruct an Egyptian 'broad collar' from its component parts. He made use of the products of the *iru weshbet,* or bead-maker; but whether this particular workman was restricted to making beads in glass and faience, in which case he would have been a specialist kind of *baba,* or whether he worked and drilled the precious stones of the *neshdy* is unknown, although the latter is sometimes found drilling beads.[14] The enormous number of beads that were produced in Egypt from all kinds of materials and which give its jewellery so much of its characteristic form and appearance, suggest that the *iru weshbet* were many and industrious.

In reliefs and paintings the jewellers are shown working side by side with metalsmiths and joiners, apparently in the same ateliers. This was probably because close supervision was exercised over all

14   Man threading
beads

15   Men making bead necklaces

those workers who had to use gold, silver and to a lesser extent bronze, in the objects they made. The gold and silver are shown being carefully weighed out and recorded for issue to the craftsmen, and doubtless they were strictly accounted for. We know that when the Pharaohs sent jewels and other valuable gifts to their brother monarchs in Asia, they took care to mention the amount of gold and silver that had gone into their making.

Pl. 148

Supplies of gold and silver appear to have been reserved for the king or the temples of the gods, such as Amun, to whom the Pharaoh had allocated gold-bearing tracts in the Eastern Desert and in Nubia. Nevertheless a certain amount of gold must have been allowed to reach private hands, for even the modest burials that have been found unrifled often yield up articles of gold in the form of amulets, beads or jewels. Gold could also be worn as gifts of the king, such as orders, decorations and parade weapons; and the bullion with which he rewarded meritorious henchmen could be made into jewels.[15] It is clear that private persons besides the Court and the gods could legitimately own articles of gold, because otherwise the robbing of tombs would have been rapidly detected, and the culprits instantly identified. It is probable, therefore, that in addition to working in the studios attached to palaces and temples, the jewellers also did a certain amount of private work in their homes, in very much the same way as the workmen of Deir el-Medina made tombs and monuments for themselves and similar clients when they were resting from their labours on the royal commissions which were their *raison d'être*.

Pls. 78–81

The tools used by the jewellers were of the simplest and most primitive kind. Their furnace was a pottery bowl upon a stand filled with glowing charcoal. Their blowpipe was a reed tipped with a clay nozzle which would need to be renewed frequently. Yet even with such a crude instrument it would have been possible to raise the temperature of a metal object heated on the brazier to a critical point in selected areas sufficiently high to make hard solders melt and run; and even to fuse the metal being worked if insufficient skill was exercised. It is clear that the craftsman could have had only a very

16 Man at a brazier

imperfect control of the heat, and it is astonishing that he achieved so much with such primitive implements. Nevertheless he was well aware of the different melting points of various solders and selected them with the size and nature of the job in view (see pp. 97-98). When a larger mass of metal had to be melted, a squad of men would bring

Fig. 13   their several pipes to bear upon the fire beneath a clay crucible; by the time of the New Kingdom, however, a blast furnace had been intro-

Fig. 17   duced worked by leather bellows actuated by the feet and cords similar to that used by native smiths in Africa in recent times.[16] Metal had to be melted in such crucibles either in order to convert gold dust, ingots or scrap into larger masses that could be subsequently beaten into sheets, or to provide a pour for casting into moulds of clay. The crucibles were lifted off the fire by two springy rods, presumably green sticks, clamped at both ends.

Gold and silver were hammered by polished pebbles held in the hand; and simple as this tool may appear, it would have been entirely effective, the domed end of the stone having the same expanding impact as the collet head of a modern raising hammer, while the flat faces could be used for planishing. The stakes on which vessels are

17   Blast furnace

shown in the process of shaping must have been of wood; so are the blocks on which gold and silver are being beaten into leaf. Perhaps such blocks were covered with skin to deaden the jarring effect of beating with a stone held in the hollow of the hand on an unresilient surface.

Such simple tools are the only ones shown in the hands of metal workers in the reliefs and paintings. Nevertheless in New York there are two hammer heads of identical shape, one in bronze and the other in limestone, similar to a modern blacksmith's hammer with a flat surface at the proximal end and a tapered wedge-shaped cutting edge at the distal.[17] It is most likely that the limestone specimen, at least, was used for working soft metals such as gold.

The place of the modern file was taken by abrasive stones of various degrees of fineness, made from sandstone and quartzite. Such implements used with fine quartz sand strained through the mesh of cloths of varying degrees of coarseness could also be used for polishing stones chipped into shape for inlays.

The ancient craftsman must have been considerably handicapped by the lack of an effective cutting device such as shears for trimming and shaping metal, which had to be punched with a bronze or copper chisel. Holes were usually made by pressing an awl into gold or silver sheet, though a bow-drill was used for drilling stones. The tongs *Figs. 12, 16* shown in the hands of workmen seated before their braziers were almost certainly of bronze or copper. Despite such crude and imprecise tools, the Egyptian jeweller achieved results which are very seldom less than commendable; such marvels of craftsmanship as the Dahshur and Lahun treasures are truly astonishing.

CHAPTER FIVE

Techniques

METALS

It is evident that with the crude tools at their command, only techniques of the simplest kind could have been employed by the Egyptian jewellers. The standards they achieved in their craftsmanship were dependent more upon skill of hand, the qualities of their raw materials and the time taken to complete a job than the precision and effectiveness of their implements. The settings of their jewels were normally made in precious metals, gold, electrum and, to a lesser extent, silver; and the processes employed by the jeweller are inseparable from those used by contemporary metalworkers.

As we have emphasized in the previous chapter, the methods of Egyptian metal workers appear to have been those in common use throughout the Near East. While the large deposits of gold in the deserts of Egypt and Nubia must first have been exploited by the natives of the region, there was probably always some opportunity for foreign techniques and styles to be introduced, particularly during the upheavals of the Hyksos invasions of the eighteenth century BC, when ancient states were modelled on new lines and new principalities appeared with fresh demands for the old luxury of jewellery and the trappings of sovereignty. In the New Kingdom, foreign princesses with their retinues of experts entered the harims of the Pharaohs as part of the diplomacy of the time.[1] Such influences are probably

Pls. 48, 55, 59, 68   responsible for inducing some scholars to see Helladic and Syrian influences in the metalwork of the period, particularly in that found in Lower Egypt.[2] The explanation may well be that the metalwork of the entire area shows a generic similarity in its techniques and styles, though it appears to be more of Egyptian inspiration than any other.[3]

The difference between the techniques of the jewellers and the metal-smiths is one of degree rather than kind. Raising and sinking metal plates upon stakes so as to hammer out beaker or dish shapes would indeed seldom have to be practised by the jeweller, but casting, repoussé, chasing and soldering would be among the skills he would daily be called upon to exercise. Here to some extent his burdens were lightened by his use of gold that was generally of a high carat, ranging from 17 to 22.[4] Such metal is soft and malleable and has a higher melting point than gold alloyed with greater amounts of silver and copper. It allows solders to be used for joining various components of the gold setting without incurring too great a risk of fusing the metal being worked; and this was important where primitive blowpipes and braziers were used which could not control temperatures to any critical extent.

Gold received in the form of rings or bags of assorted granules had first to be made into sheets for most jewellery and this would be done by fusing the dust or ingots into larger masses in the blast furnace, pouring the melt onto a flat surface and hammering it out to a sheet of the required thickness. The gold beating would have the effect of making the metal hard and brittle, particularly if it were of a lower carat, and unless this springy effect was required it would have to be reheated from time to time in order to anneal it. In the absence of any tool resembling shears, the gold sheets would have had to be cut by scoring several times with a sharp implement such as a flint or hardened copper chisel, and, if the metal was thick, by bending it to and fro until it fractured along the score-marks. In the case of less extensive cuts or more complicated forms, the plate was trimmed to the required shape by means of a copper or bronze chisel, tapped with a wooden mallet.

Gold of a high carat is sufficiently malleable to be worked with tools of bone or even hardwood,[5] and these may very well have been used for repoussé and chasing. For these processes, the plate with the design drawn upon it was mounted upon a bed of some firm yet yielding substance such as wax, or a mixture of wax, resin and mud, upon a board. What appears to be the remains of such a 'pitch-block', with a cast of the metal sheet that was once worked upon it, was found by the Germans in a sculptor's studio at Amarna in 1913–14.[6] The outlines and interior linear detail could be pressed into the mounted metal with a tool of bronze or bone by the repoussé method. Such lines would appear on the reverse side of the plate as raised contours. Hollows hammered into the metal by means of a hardwood, bone or metal punch with a polished end that could be slid over the surface between each hammer blow, would appear on the reverse as raised domes. Repoussé is virtually the complementary process to chasing, being worked on the back of the plate instead of its face. By alternating the two processes the metal can be pressed and hammered into relief which, if necessary, may be more than half-round. At the same time fine detail can be indicated and sharpness and precision achieved in the drawing. The gold reverses of the pectorals from Dahshur and Lahun were worked by these processes.

Pls. 73, 74, 76

Engraving, another technique of the goldsmith, involves the ploughing-out of a furrow in the metal with a sharp point. In view of the absence of iron or steel tools in Egypt until the Late Period, there has been some speculation about the nature of the burin used, and flakes of chert, obsidian and other hard and brittle stones capable of being chipped to a sharp point have been suggested.[7] Stone tools of this type may have been used for carving and engraving hard substances such as ivory; but engraving weakens metal by scooping out trenches in its surface and is impossible on material which is thin in section. It would appear, therefore, that the Egyptians engraved metal only when iron became common. Until then, fine detail was added by delicate chasing.

Besides working flat sheet into raised relief by repoussé and chasing, it was also possible to press, hammer or burnish thin metal into dies cut in lead, stone, wood or pottery. Such a method was employed where a great number of simple standard shapes were required, as for instance in metal beads or elements used in the stringing of collars or girdles. It would seem that hollow metal beads were

Pl. 86

53   Gold flies of Queen Ah-hotpe, from Western Thebes

54   Armlet of Queen Ah-hotpe in the form of a vulture, from Western Thebes

55 Falcon Collar of Queen Ah-hotpe, from Western Thebes

56 Scarab and chain of Queen Ah-hotpe, from Western Thebes

57 Rigid bracelet of Queen Ah-hotpe, from Western Thebes

58 Gold bracelet of Queen Ah-hotpe, from Western Thebes

60 Wall-painting of royal concubines, tomb of Menna,
Thebes

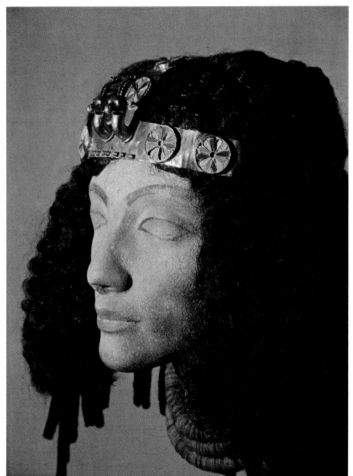

◁ 59 The 'Stag' circlet
of a queen, from
a Delta site

61 Gazelle circlet of a
queen of Tuthmosis III,
from Thebes

62 Long head–dress of a queen of Tuthmosis III, from Thebes

63   Belt and fish girdle of a queen of Tuthmosis III, from Thebes

64   Gold rigid bracelets of queens of Tuthmosis III, from Thebes

65 Falcon Collar of a queen of Tuthmosis III, from Thebes

71   Broad Collar of King Smenkh-ka-re, from Thebes

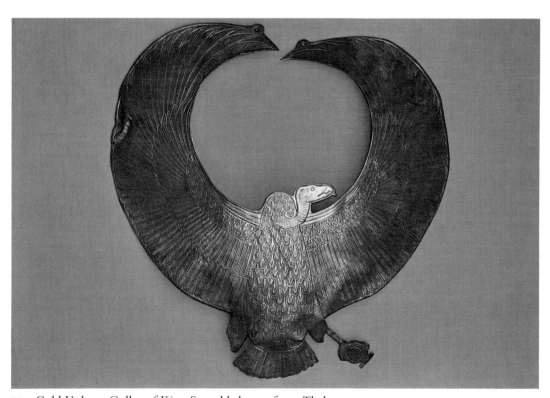

72   Gold Vulture Collar of King Smenkh-ka-re, from Thebes

68 Ear-plugs and ear-rings of the New Kingdom

69 Rings of the Amarna Period

70 Rings of Amenophis III, the Aten and Akhenaten

67　Wall-painting of orchestra and dancers, tomb of Neb-Amun, from Thebes

66 Broad Collar with flower terminals of a queen of Tuthmosis III, from Thebes

made by working sheet into a die cut with a bowl-like depression, *Pls.* 14, 22
perforating the hemispheres so formed with their thread holes,
trimming their edges and soldering them together along their adjacent large circles. Where a solid result was required, the two halves
of such shells were filled with a fine compact clay before soldering *Cf. Pl.* 78
could take place.

As the complementary process, sheet gold could be worked
over a pottery, wood, stone or metal positive formed as a core that
could be withdrawn, provided there were no undercuts, to leave a
shell of metal reproducing the likeness of the original, but larger by
the thickness of the metal sheet. Such a process was used where the
shape was more complex and difficult to cut in intaglio in a die. It is *Cf. Pl.* 46
probable that the heads of the goddess Bat on the mirrors and caskets
of the Lahun and Dahshur jewels were made by this method. The
Egyptians as early as the Archaic Period were able to make copper
statues by hammering sheets of metal over a wooden core retained
within[8] and such work must have made them familiar with the
moulding effects they could obtain by this means. In the case of gold
shells made by the same method, additional detail and depth could
be added by chasing and repoussé.

The Egyptians were also familiar with the modelling effects of
stamping moulds into wet clay sealings, and must have tried to secure
a similar effect by interposing a thin sheet of gold between the stamp
and a soft impressionable substance such as clay, and exerting additional pressure by striking the stamp with a hammer. The uniform
results so achieved by the operation of the same stamp, could also, of
course, have been enhanced by chasing the metal impression. It would
seem that the gold amulets used for funerary purposes, and generally
of a rather simple and flimsy construction, were made by this method.

Strips could be cut from metal sheet by scoring or by cutting
with the chisel, and if they were made sufficiently thin would assume
the form of a wire triangular or square in section. This raises one of
the problems of ancient technology, whether the Egyptians knew
how to draw such strips into wires of circular cross-section, or whether

18 Chisel cutting plate
into wires

they employed a technique familiar in Hellenistic times of winding a thin strip of gold upon a mandrel, such as a length of thread, subsequently withdrawn, in the same way as paper drinking-straws are made.[9] The tube so formed could be made smaller in diameter by tighter coiling. Another and easier method more generally employed in the Hellenistic age is 'block-twisting', by which a strip of metal of square or rectangular cross-section was twisted about its major axis, resulting in a solid wire with a screw thread of variable pitch.[10] The preparation of such wire would require frequent annealing. A finish was imparted by rolling it between flat surfaces which, if sufficiently vigorous, could almost eliminate the spiralling. The wire could be made thinner by tighter twisting and stretching.

There is no evidence that in early Pharaonic times the Egyptians made wires by these methods, though not enough examples have survived and been studied to give a proper conspectus. It has been claimed that the square-sectioned wires were made round by hammering, a process which would have been virtually impossible except in the case of thick wires. It would have been feasible to roll wire of square or triangular section between two hard flat surfaces so as to round off the corners by pressure or abrasion, only for short lengths at a time. Unfortunately, in his pictures of metalworkers in action, the ancient Egyptian did not represent the process of wire-making. While the use of the drawplate made of a hard stone, such as glazed steatite, has been postulated by several investigators such as Möller and Vernier,[11] the suggestion has been generally scouted. The Egyptian was able to drill hardstone beads for threading upon

Pl. 49 wires as well as linen fibres, and it does not seem improbable that he would have noticed in time the effect of forcing a bead drilled with a circular hole over a wire of square or triangular section, especially as the Egyptian drill would have made a hole of conical shape. Arthur H. Kopp, the ill-fated chemist of the Metropolitan Museum of Art,

Pl. 6 noted in the case of the gold wire circlet of Seneb-tisi that 'microscopic examination showed . . . plain evidence that this wire had been cut from sheet and then drawn – square edges are seen here and there, and even shear marks at right angles to the wire axis, while longitudinal streaks plainly show evidence of drawing.'[12]

The pulling of square or triangular sectioned wire through a bead would have been more of a smoothing action than a drawing one, and it may well be that the bead was rubbed up and down the wire and not the wire pulled through the bead. If the hole was not exactly circular at its egress, but had been broken through by drilling from one side only, an irregularity could have caused the striations that are sometimes seen in these wires. In the New Kingdom, however, when new processes may have been introduced, the block-twisting method appears on the scene to supplement the rolling and smoothing processes of making wires. The first evidence can be seen on an ear-plug of Amarna date which reveals that both techniques   Pl. 68 were in use on the same object; the braided wires having apparently been made by block-twisting, the plain ones by rolling or possibly smoothing.

Long lengths of wire were seldom required for Egyptian jewels, the circlet of Seneb-tisi being a notable exception. When a continuous length of wire was required, it was made by soldering shorter lengths together. The imperfect joins of such a length might be the 'shear marks' observed by Arthur Kopp. For most of his work the Egyptian jeweller required only short lengths of wire, the main need for which was in the manufacture of chains. For these, wire was coiled upon a rod of suitable diameter and cut longitudinally to produce a number of penannular rings which could then be inter-linked before soldering the ends of each ring together. The resulting chain was, of course, very simple. A more complicated and stronger chain was made by   *Cf.* Pl. 133 soldering each penannular ring into a continuous circle, pressing it into an elongated figure-8 shape and bending it up into a stirrup which could be looped through another.[13] Such chains tend to have a square cross-section and are sometimes known as square or loop-in-loop   Pls. 56, 140 chains. The loops may be doubled, quadrupled or even sextupled by threading each link through the ends of the two or more preceding links. The resulting chain is columnar in shape with a woven herringbone effect that has frequently encouraged the erroneous belief that they have been plaited.

Another method of making wires was by soldering granules into given lengths and straightening the wire so formed by rolling it Pl. 68 between two flat surfaces. The ear-plug from Amarna shows examples of such wire, as does some of the goldwork from the tomb of Pl. 112 Tut-ankh-amun. Beaded wires made by this method are best treated under granular work below.

For constructing the metal settings of his various jewels, the Egyptian had to join pieces together with hard solders, and several Fig. 16 pictures of the goldsmith sitting at his brazier with blowpipe in mouth and tongs in hand show him at this exacting task. That the Egyptians knew how to join metal with hard solder by the Fourth Dynasty at the latest is clear from the bed canopy which belonged to Queen Hetep-her-es (c. 2600 BC), since its copper sockets were formed by bending sheet copper into a cylinder and soldering the overlapping joints with a silver alloy.[14]

A group of five gold fishes found in the coffin of an infant in a Pl. 78 Middle Kingdom grave at Haraga[15] clearly reveals that the Egyptian goldsmith was familiar with solders of different melting points and chose them carefully according to the size and nature of the job. These fish pendants are graduated in length from 4 cm. for the largest to 1·5 cm. for the smallest. They have survived in various states of preservation, the largest being in perfect condition and the smallest in a state of total disintegration. It is clear that each was made of two shells formed either in a mould, or more probably over a wood or steatite positive. The half of each fish was filled with a finely levigated clay, the fins and tail inserted along the medial line, and solder run around the join. In the case of the largest fish there were sufficient heat-losses from its more extensive surface area to ensure that the ancient craftsman with his crude blowpipe could only just reach the temperature necessary to melt the gold solder used; but in the case of the smaller fishes, no such control was possible and he was in danger of fusing the thin shells almost at the same time as the solder

73 Reverse of the first pectoral
of Princess Sit-Hathor-Yunet,
from Lahun

74 Reverse of the second pectoral
of Princess Sit-Hathor-Yunet,
from Lahun

75 Bracelets of Princess Sit-Hathor-Yunet,
from Lahun

76 Reverse of the second pectoral of Queen Mereret, from Dahshur

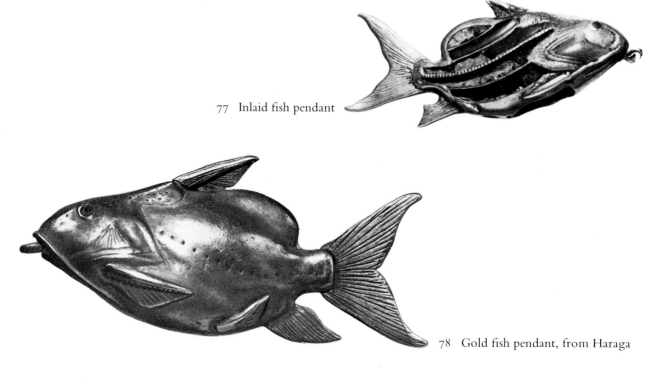

77 Inlaid fish pendant

78 Gold fish pendant, from Haraga

79 Gold shell of Sesostris III, from Rikka

80. 81 Front and back views
of a Middle Kingdom pectoral, from Rikka

82 Uraeus on the Intef crown, from Thebes

83 Rear view of the Intef crown, from Thebes

84 Bead bracelets of queens of Tuthmosis III with cats, from Thebes

85 Inscribed gold anklets of queens of Tuthmosis III, from Thebes

86   Necklaces of three of the queens of Tuthmosis III, from Thebes

87–89   Bracelet plaques of Amenophis III

90   Faience bracelet of Amenophis III

itself. For the second largest fish, therefore, he chose a silver solder with a melting point well below that of the gold shells. At the time of discovery the solder which had flashed along the seam and over part of the fins and tail had changed to an easily visible purple 'horn-silver'. The other fishes in the group had been soldered with alloys of even lower melting points, containing copper, judging from the green deposits left on the goldwork. In the case of the two smallest fishes this poorer solder had decayed completely and the shells had fallen apart revealing the method of construction.

Whether the goldsmith made solders artificially or used less rich metals, which he distinguished by colour, to join nobler metals is problematical. Presumably he began in earliest times by empirical means to discover that some types of naturally occurring gold would fuse at a lower temperature than others; but it is almost certain that the making of bronze would have familiarized him with the ability to lower the fusing point of a metal by adding other metals or substances to the melt. Certainly by the Amarna Period he was producing a copper-gold alloy that could hardly have occurred in nature,[16] and some of the goldwork from the tomb of Tut-ankh-amun suggests that he was deliberately debasing gold by adding copper or silver, since the objects show patchy tarnishing and corrosion.

Pl. 69

Pls. 95, 96

The hard soldering of metals, whether with natural or artificial alloys, would have required the use of an oxide-removing flux to achieve success. In modern times borax is generally used for such purposes but there is no evidence that this mineral was used in ancient times. Deposits of borax have not been recorded in modern Egypt. The nearest plentiful supplies are found in Turkey and Tuscany,[17] but it is doubtful whether borax was traded from such remote sites to Egypt in antiquity. No name for the mineral has been identified in ancient Egyptian lexicography; nor has the element boron been traced in analyses of ancient Egyptian materials. If borax had been used as a flux, it seems strange that no traces of it have been found in Egyptian glass or faience, in which, however, natron plays an important chemical role as a flux and binder. Natron, a mixture of sodium carbonate and bi-carbonate, with other sodium salts, occurs abundantly in Egypt and had such a multitude of uses that it was regarded as a magic substance. It is improbable that the fluxing and de-oxidizing qualities of natron in soldering would not have been discovered in antiquity. In point of fact, the writer has found no difficulty in joining pieces of silver with silver solder using a mixture of sodium carbonate and bi-carbonate in place of the usual borax. It has the advantage that it does not sputter like borax. Such a flux must *Cf.* Pl. 78 have been used to silver-solder the second largest of the Haraga fishes, since solder had run onto the fins and tail following the course of surplus flux and had not subsequently been cleaned off, perhaps because it was less visible when new than when it had been converted into purple-brown horn-silver.

While it is clear, therefore, that the ancient Egyptians could solder metal with alloys of copper and silver, using natron as a flux, some doubt exists about the means they employed for soldering their goldwork with gold-rich solders. In ancient gold jewellery, the joins between the various components are usually undetectable. In the group of gold fishes from Haraga, for instance, while the silver/copper soldered joints are visible in the smaller specimens, the two halves of the largest fish are joined by a gold solder that cannot be distinguished from the gold of the shells and fins. If the join had been made by a gold alloy with a lower melting-point than the component parts, the solder would have been visible by its different colour, however slight, and however carefully any surplus might have been cleaned away, since after the lapse of nearly four millennia a distinct patina would have had a chance to develop.

This lack of any distinction in colour between the gold of ancient objects and their soldered joints has been ascribed by some authorities[18] to the welding together of the various parts, a technique which would have been quite impossible with the crude tools in use at the time. Other writers have suggested 'surface enrichment' to account for the uniformity in colour.[19] When gold alloys have been buried for any length of time, electrolytic action with salts in damp soils results in the disappearance of the baser metals in favour of the nobler. It has also been postulated that the ancients employed mild acids such as vinegar to achieve surface enrichment quickly by artificial means.[20] Such treatment would have resulted in the pitting of the areas containing the displaced metals, whereas no such effects are discernible, even under strong magnification. Moreover, goldwork which has survived in dry conditions without contact with damp soils, reveals the same qualities.

There seems little doubt to the writer that the ancients soldered their goldwork by the process known as colloidal hard soldering, which was re-discovered in recent times by H. A. P. Littledale[21] in seeking a means of reproducing the effects of Etruscan granular and filigree work without flooding the grains and wires with solder. Mrs P. F. Davidson, Research Associate of the Brooklyn Museum, has shown that a simplified version of Littledale's process results in a bond between various gold parts which 'if properly done has no peer in strength'.[22] In colloidal hard soldering, ground copper carbonate, probably in ancient Egypt in the form of powdered malachite so commonly used as an eye-cosmetic, is mixed with gum or glue and this adhesive is employed to stick the grains or wire into place, or to coat the adjacent edges of the parts to be joined. The work is then heated on the charcoal brazier with the assistance of the blowpipe on those areas which have to be raised to the highest temperatures. At $100°C$ the carbonate changes to copper oxide; by $600°C$ the adhesive has become completely carbonized and at $850°C$ the carbon combines with the oxygen in the copper oxide and vaporizes as carbon dioxide, leaving the merest traces of copper adhering to the gold parts. At about $880°C$ a curious phenomenon occurs: the gold in contact with the copper melts to form a welded joint, whereas both gold and copper melt at nearly the same temperature well above this point viz $1083°$ and $1063°C$ respectively. The process had great advantages for the ancient craftsmen. There was no decrepitation of flux to throw pallets of solder off the job, and the various parts were already stuck together by the dried adhesive before heat was applied.

All that required to be done, once the mixture had been correctly prepared and applied, was careful heating over the bed of glowing charcoal. The work could subsequently be heated up a number of times to affix other elements, without the risk of unfastening joints that had previously been made. Mrs Davidson has used the technique to 'fasten granules to granules, granules to sheet gold, sheet gold to sheet gold, wire to sheet gold and every other possible combination of grains, sheet and filigree.' She has further found that it is possible to exclude the copper carbonate from the adhesive if the gold to be joined already has a sufficiently high percentage of copper.[23]

The process is particularly suitable for gold, though claims have been made that it will also work for silver. For copper itself hard solder with fluxes must have been used. Although the ancient Egyptians knew of tin by the New Kingdom at least, and had smelted lead in small amounts from predynastic times, soft solder was not developed in antiquity for jewellery or fine work in metal.[24]

Colloidal hard soldering was used to join granules together to form beaded wires and these were subsequently rolled between flat surfaces to straighten them. Increasing the pressure during rolling has the effect of squeezing the grains into cylindrical or spool shapes.[25] Ancient Egyptian beaded wires, which were introduced in the Amarna Period, do not show the elaboration of shapes which are so characteristic of later Hellenistic work, and evidently rolling was limited to straightening a crooked row of granules soldered together. Pl. 68   Nevertheless, in the ear-plug from Amarna the effect of unequal pressure on the plates rolling over the wires has resulted in the distortion of the granules into near spool shapes in places, and it is interesting to see the emergence at this moment of time of an accidental effect that was later intentionally exploited.

Granules of uniform size are made today by such processes as snipping strips of metal into equal squares, or winding wire over a mandrel and cutting the coil so as to produce rings of equal size. These particles are then heated until they fuse into globules. Similar methods have been postulated for antiquity; but such processes,

92   Vulture pectoral of Tut-ankh-amun, from Thebes ▷

93   Winged scarab pectoral of Tut-ankh-amun, from Thebes ▷

94 Scarab pectoral of Tut-ankh-amun, with Isis and Nephthys, from Thebes

95 *Djed*-column pectoral of Tut-ankh-amun, with Isis and Nephthys, from Thebes

96 Osiris pectoral of Tut–ankh–amun, with Edjo and Nekhebet, from Thebes

97 Nut pectoral of Tut–ankh–amun, from Thebes

98 Winged scarab pectoral of Tut-ankh-amun, with Isis and Nephthys, from Thebes

99, 100 Coronation pectoral and counterpoise of Tut-ankh-amun, from Thebes

102 Pendant of Tut-ankh-amun in the form of a vulture, from Thebes

103 Vulture pectoral of Tut-ankh-amun representing Nekhebet, from Thebes

◁ 101 Pectoral of Tut-ankh-amun with moon bark, necklace
and counterpoise, from Thebes

105 Bead stole and vulture pendant of Tut-ankh-amun, from Thebes

◁ 104 Scarab and falcon pendants of Tut-ankh-amun, from Thebes

106 Rebus pectoral of Tut-ankh-amun, from Thebes

107 Scarab pendant and two clasps of Tut-ankh-amun, from Thebes

108 Counterpoise of Tut-ankh-amun, with figure of Eternity, from Thebes

109 Two scarab bracelets of Tut-ankh-amun, from Thebes

110 Massive scarab bracelet of Tut-ankh-amun, from Thebes

which are simple with modern tools, would have been found difficult by the ancient craftsman. He had, however, plentiful supplies of ready-made granules to hand in the bags of gold dust in which much of the gold tribute reached him. All he needed to do to obtain grains of uniform size was to sift the contents of such bags through screens of different mesh. Two or more such granules could be fused together to obtain larger globules.

During the New Kingdom the Egyptians made a bead by soldering five or more grains into a ring around a central hole.[26] When these were threaded together, they intermeshed to produce what looks like a flexible reticulated tube of solid gold. Examples have been found in the tombs of three queens of Tuthmosis III and of Tut-ankh-amun. Hollow ball beads were also found there decorated with granular work. The earliest appearance of such techniques in Egypt, however, is found in the treasure of the Princess Khnumet from Dahshur and has a decided Asiatic look with its star-shaped medallions. The butterfly motif with its somewhat Aegean echo had appeared much earlier in the jewellery of Queen Hetep-her-es;[27] and in the absence of all personal jewellery of the Old Kingdom, it would be rash to assert that granular work was not introduced until the Middle Kingdom. Nevertheless there are good grounds for believing it to be of Asiatic origin, since the goldwork found by Woolley in the royal cemetery of Ur and dated to *c.* 2550 BC already shows familiar designs in granules.[28] It may well be that with the more intimate contacts between Egypt and Asia in the Twelfth Dynasty, new techniques were introduced by immigrants and adopted by native goldsmiths.

There is less doubt about the origins of the most characteristic feature of Egyptian jewellery, its cloisonné-work in which strips of metal were bent to shape, placed on edge and soldered to base plates so as to form cells or cloisons. The cells were then set with coloured inlays cut to shape and cemented in position, the entire surface being subsequently polished. This technique was known from the early Old Kingdom at the latest, for fragmentary dummy vessels have been

Pls. 86, 121, 122

Pl. 29

Pl. 3

excavated from the ruins of the mortuary temple of King Nefer-ir-ka-re (*obit. c.* 2460 BC) which imitate originals made of gold inlaid with coloured stones.[29] Scraps of jewellery found in the tomb of Queen Iput of the early Sixth Dynasty (*obit. c.* 2340 BC) include two drop beads made in cloisonné-work.[30] The technique reached its greatest perfection in the Middle Kingdom, but it is still very much in evidence in the tomb of Tut-ankh-amun where, however, short cuts were being taken in the fitting of the inlays which will be mentioned in the next chapter.

Related to cloisonné-work is niello, in which an alloy of copper and silver blackened by sulphur compounds is used as a foil to raised designs in gold.[31] Examples of this technique are more characteristic of the Aegean area; and almost the only example from Egypt is the blade of the dagger of Amosis, found in the treasure of Queen Ah-hotpe, which has an inscription and animal designs inlaid gold against a black composition centre-rib on each side of the blade.[32]

The remaining technique of metal-working which the Egyptians had fully mastered was casting. This was not often employed in jewellery-making since stampings and mouldings in sheet metal gave adequate and more economical results. Nevertheless, there was no alternative to casting in the case of certain parts of objects or of entire

Pl. 103 jewels. The head of the vulture pectoral of Tut-ankh-amun, for instance, must have been cast, since carving and filing it out of the mass would have been very wasteful of precious gold.

Such pieces were doubtless cast by the *cire perdue* method, the model being worked in beeswax, fitted with a sprue and the whole invested with fine clay. When this had been carefully dried and heated to a high temperature the wax would burn off, allowing gold melted in a crucible to be poured into the cavity. Statuettes and similar small articles would be cast solid, but the Egyptian in the New Kingdom, at least, could also cast larger objects by the *cire perdue* method on a core retained within by chaplets of copper.[33]

Pl. 1 Another method of casting solid was by using an open mould. Hollow casts can also be made in a closed mould by pouring in the melt, rinsing it around the cavity and draining off the surplus before it solidifies; but there is no evidence for such an advanced technique in the ancient world. Such moulds would need to have been made of a suitable stone such as steatite with cavities cut *in intaglio*. A half of a bi-partite mould in gabbro in the Metropolitan Museum may have been used for bronze casting.[34] A limestone open mould in the same collection was probably used for casting objects in glass or faience rather than metal.[35] It is possible, however, that such moulds were used to cast standard wax blanks from which repetitive work, such as the heavy signet rings of the New Kingdom, had subsequently to be cast by the *cire perdue* method.

Pls. 69, 70

NON-METALS

Egyptian jewellery has conveniently been classified into hoop jewellery, which consists essentially of metal hoops such as finger-rings, anklets, bracelets, circlets and the like; and bead jewellery, which comprises necklaces, girdles, collars, head-dresses, bracelets and anklets.[36] Pectorals, amulets and pendants may be regarded for the purposes of this classification as more elaborate beads. The special contribution of Egypt to the jeweller's art was its bead jewellery. No other nation of antiquity produced such an enormous wealth of beads in so many different shapes and substances, and used them not only in single and multiple strings but threaded in warps and wefts to form patterned textiles; or sewed them on linen or papyrus backing to make such articles of dress as belts, aprons and sandals.

Beads which are found in Egypt as early as the Neolithic period were first made of natural objects such as pebbles, seeds, shells, teeth, horns and bones which had some amuletic significance. But aesthetics reinforced magic when objects were fashioned out of materials chosen for their appearance as much as for their numinous power. The earliest of these were pebbles and crystals that could be shaped, drilled and polished to thread upon a string. A factory for making stone beads found at Kerma above the Third Cataract of the Nile, though dating to the Twelfth Dynasty, doubtless shows techniques

19   Man drilling
carnelian

which had long been traditional.[37] The first stage of the process was to select pebbles (e.g. of carnelian or jasper) or crystals (e.g. of amethyst or garnet) of an appropriate size and shape, or to break up larger stones to obtain such pieces roughly chipped to shape. They were then drilled, sometimes from one point only, but often from opposite poles when the hole began to wander from its proper axis. Some doubt exists as to the type of drill used. In prehistoric times it may have been a stalk fed with an abrasive powder and rotated between the palms of the hands. The 'wobbly drill'[38] with its flint borer used for hollowing out stone vases does not appear to have been used for beads. An enigmatic scene in a relief dated to the Late Old Kingdom *Fig. 19* shows large blocks of carnelian being worked by an instrument, apparently of wood, perhaps a development of the hand rotated stalk. For the most part, however, the drill in common use was the bow-drill. Its point was usually of copper fed with an abrasive powder such as crushed flint, chert, stone-dust from the beads themselves, or fine quartz sand; but there seems some evidence that the borers could also be of flint or chert, perhaps reflecting a traditional practice dating back to prehistoric times.[39] Scenes in New Kingdom tombs show lapidaries operating three drill-stocks at once with the same bow, but though it has been claimed that the feat is possible it seems more *Fig. 15* likely that the operation represented is polishing rather than accurate boring.[40]

The rough perforated beads were then ground to a better finish by rolling them between flat rubbers of an abrasive stone such as quartzite; or in the case of cylindrical beads or several disk beads threaded on to an axle, by rubbing them in grooves ploughed out of gritty stone blocks. They may also have been finally polished by jamming them on the points of a bow-drill and rotating them in suitable recesses in a wooden block fed with an abrasive mixture of fine quartz sand and oil or water.

The art of the bead-maker reached a high point of achievement *Pl. 47* in the Middle Kingdom. From this period stone beads have survived of minute size and extraordinary fineness in which perforations of

III Nekhebet collar of Tut-ankh-amun, from Thebes

112 Bracelets of Tut-ankh-amun, from Thebes

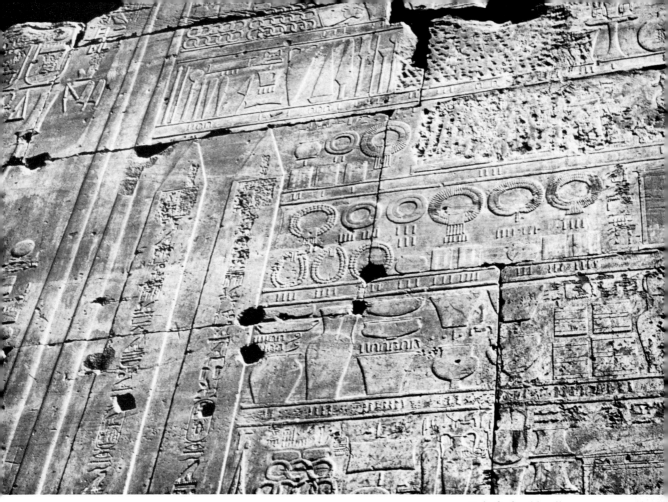

119 Relief of gold collars
offered by Tuthmosis III at Karnak

118 Presentation of gold collars
by Akhenaten and Nefert-iti,
drawing of a relief in a tomb at Amarna

The investiture of Har-em-hab with gold collars, relief from his tomb at Saqqara great length occur. How such beads were made is unknown but it is to be suspected that the hole must have been drilled first and the body afterwards rubbed away till the desired degree of thinness had been obtained.

The constant search for a convenient substance from which hard blue and green beads could be easily made was partly successful when the Egyptians discovered how to coat steatite (soapstone) with a green or blue vitreous alkaline glaze as early as the Badarian period of the prehistoric age (*c.* 4000 BC).[41] Steatite, which occurs in several places in Egypt, can easily be worked since it is very fine-grained and soft enough to be marked by the finger nail. It is eminently suitable for carving into such objects as statuettes, vases, amulets and beads. On being heated in the glazing oven it does not change or fracture but becomes dehydrated, in which state it is hard enough to scratch glass.[42] The working of steatite into glazed beads, while not difficult, is tedious and time-consuming, and except for the more complicated shapes steatite was replaced by mass-produced faience beads.

White disk beads were made from shells, particularly that of the ostrich egg, which were broken into pieces of convenient size and trimmed roughly circular, then drilled, threaded on a stiff core and rubbed to shape in the same way as stone disk beads were made. Such shell disks exist from the Neolithic period and never completely lost favour, though they were replaced in the Eighteenth Dynasty by similarly shaped beads made of white faience.[43]

The greater proportion of ancient Egyptian beads, however, are made of faience (see p. 35) which was introduced in the predynastic period. According to Petrie and Reisner, such beads were made on an axis, perhaps of thread, which would be burnt out in the firing, leaving a hole.[44] Disk beads, ring beads and tubular beads were made by coating the axis with the body-paste, rolling the long cylinder so formed on a flat surface and scoring it with a knife into sections of different lengths, depending upon what kind of bead was required. Other shapes, such as ball beads, were rolled between the hands and perforated while still soft with a stiff point such as a needle-like wire.

The beads were then dried, coated with glaze, if indeed glaze had not been mixed with the paste, and fired, the smaller specimens often being fused to the condition of translucent frit.

The vast majority of faience beads are blue or green in colour; but black, red, yellow and white beads were also produced, especially in the New Kingdom. In addition to making beads of simple geometrical forms, the Egyptians could press faience into moulds to make beads of more complex shape, such as pear-shaped drop beads, hieroglyphs, figurines, leaf and flower forms. Ring beads were attached to one or more points of the larger beads at the final glazing and are the means of stringing them into collars and bracelets. In the Amarna Period, when faience and glass manufacture reached a high degree of perfection, leaf, flower-petal and fruit forms were cast in polychrome faience as elements in the elaborate floral collars and fillets that replaced the more ephemeral archetype worn on festal occasions.

Pl. 125

The latest material from which beads were made was glass, introduced in quantity during the New Kingdom. Petrie, who had an excellent opportunity of studying the manufacture of glass from the remains of the factory he found at Tell el-Amarna, reports that the usual method of making beads was by winding drawn-out threads of molten glass upon a copper wire which contracted on cooling and could be withdrawn.[45] Threads of different colours could evidently be used in the same bead; and drop shapes, as well as spherical, cylindrical and barrel beads, were produced by this method. Glass, too, could be pressed into moulds and treated very much as a more brilliant kind of faience. Some modest jewellery was also produced at this time entirely in glass, such as ear-studs, and ear-rings made of two differently coloured glass canes twisted together to form diagonally striped rods.

Pl. 68

A decline of skill in the manufacture and manipulation of glass is evident in Egypt after the end of the Eighteenth Dynasty, and as a material it virtually disappears after the fall of the New Kingdom with the destruction of the Late Bronze Age civilization of the Near

East.[46] Glass-making in Egypt was not revived until Ptolemaic times after Alexander the Great had founded Alexandria with its cosmopolitan population and trades in the fourth century BC.

The Egyptians learnt very early to combine strings of beads into chokers, bracelets and anklets by means of spacer beads. These were in effect perforated bars of bone or ivory or wood, often covered with gold leaf, or of faience or metal interspersed along the threads at intervals to keep the beads in position as flexible bands of ornament instead of a sagging tangle of strings. Bead work, so threaded, could be made into the pattern of the block-border so dear to the sensibility of the Egyptian artist as a decorative motif.

20   Chokers

A special kind of spacer was the collar terminal, usually in the form of a flat faience or stone lunette with diagonal holes on its straight edge through which the various strings of beads could be anchored. Other holes at the opposite point of the terminal took the tie-strings by which the collar was secured. In the funerary Broad Collars the end-pieces are often in the form of a falcon's head; and the most elaborate examples are of gold inlaid with stone or substitutes.

Pls. 8, 10, 66

Pls. 7, 11, 55, 65

The making of stone beads was a routine if exacting task: the more expert lapidaries must have specialized in the cutting, fitting and polishing of the inlays that went into the making of the cloisonné jewellery which is the chief glory of Egyptian decorative art. It is probable that a fragment of jasper, carnelian, turquoise, felspar or lapis lazuli, left over from bead-making, was selected as near to the required shape as possible and chipped and rubbed so as to fit the appropriate cell exactly. It was cemented into position with resin mixed with a calcareous filler,[47] such as powdered limestone or gypsum, presumably applied in a molten state since an oleo-resin would have taken a long time to dry out and harden. The cements were often tinted to match the colour of the inlays, but in the Dahshur and Lahun jewels the filler now appears as a white plaster which may have lost its pigments and organic adhesives. When the inlays had all been fitted carefully, the entire face of the jewel almost certainly would have received a final polish.

Inlay work must have been a highly skilled occupation and it is very probable that the craftsmen would have sought ways of securing the desired result by less laborious means. The substitution of green and blue frit for the rare and costly turquoise, felspar, and lapis lazuli must have eased their tasks somewhat, since this material could have been cast near to the required shapes and sizes. The introduction of niello suggests that the jeweller was striving to find a plastic material that could be easily and quickly inserted in the cloisons and fill them exactly without incurring long and tedious labour in the process. The substitution of glass for natural stones in the New Kingdom gave the craftsman a means of casting his inlays direct in the cloisons, since all he would need to do was to pack powdered glass into the cells and heat it up until it fused into a compact mass. This is virtually the process of enamelling, in which the glass at its melting point penetrates the surface of the metal and adheres closely to it.

That the ancient Egyptians knew the arts of enamelling is generally denied, despite the fact that it would have been perfectly feasible for powdered glass to be fused in the separate cells of gold cloisonné-work, since the melting-point of ancient soda-lime glass is below that of gold.[48] The presence of lead in some glass from Amarna would also assist in a proper bond between the glass and metal.[49] While it is apparent that in most of the jewels of Tut-ankh-amun, glass inlays have been used like precious stones, each piece being cut, shaped to fit its cell and cemented in position, there is at least one object which displays a different technique. This is the pectoral in the form of a
Pl. 103 vulture which may have been worn by the king in life. It is made of gold, the cloisons being inlaid with blue, green and red glass. The inlays fit their cells more tightly and accurately than is the case with the majority of jewels from the same deposit; and this and the absence of any traces of cement give them the appearance of having been fired *in situ*. The proof that this is indeed the case is to be seen in the small crater made by an air-bubble visible in most of the red glass inlays forming the lesser coverts of the wing. Blow-holes can also be seen under the microscope in one or two places in the blue glass inlays,

while the outlines of the gold ribs have a burred effect, as though the entire surface has subsequently been ground down, the inlays having shrunk in their beds on firing.[50]

This pectoral at least shows an example of cloisonné enamelling and a closer examination of other of the Tut-ankh-amun jewels might reveal that it is not unique; some of the finger rings, for instance, look as though the backgrounds of their bezels are enamelled in blue glass.

CHAPTER SIX

The Forms

The jewel worn on the head by both men and women, royalty and commoners, was the circlet, known from the captions to the coffin pictures of the Middle Kingdom as the 'boatman's circlet'.[1] In its most rudimentary form this appears to have been a chaplet, woven of water-weed plucked from the river verges, that was placed on the brow to confine the hair. The strong north wind that so often prevails over the waterway in the Nile Valley is very apt to blow the boatman's hair into his eyes, and the meaning of the phrase is obvious. In time this vegetable prototype was translated into a more permanent metal version and the gold wire circlet of the House-mistress Senebtisi from Lisht is a Twelfth Dynasty simplified version of such a chaplet. The almost contemporary crown of the Princess Khnumet from Dahshur is a much more sophisticated example, in which the strands of weed have been intertwined with flowers and buds made of blue, red and green stones in gold settings.

A further development from this circlet was the diadem, originally a band of linen tied around the brow with a bow at the back, the loose ends falling on the neck. Lotus flowers and buds could be tucked into this band, especially on festal occasions. In the reliefs of the Old Kingdom there frequently appears a scene of boatmen wearing such flower-bedecked fillets and engaging in real or sham fights in their papyrus skiffs. Probably these contests have a religious significance and the circlets themselves have a primary or incidental meaning, like the Crown of Justification of Hellenistic times.[2] Certainly, the boatman's circlet became a royal crown when mounted with a uraeus or vulture, and was worn by both kings and queens.

Fig. 6

Pl. 6

Pl. 28

Pl. 17

Pls. 39, 83, 123

As a costume adjunct worn by commoners, the natural flowers were soon replaced by stylized versions in beads; while the band, its knot, and the loose ends falling as streamers, also lent themselves to interpretation as beadwork held together by spacers. Such fillets appear to be worn by the daughters of Djehuti-hotpe in a painted relief from his tomb dating to the Middle Kingdom. That the flower-bedecked chaplet had already been the inspiration for a metalwork version by at least the early Old Kingdom is shown in the painted statue of Nofret at Cairo. Here on a white band are set red and green rosettes, each with eight radiating lines from a central boss flanked by the calyx of a flower or perhaps the spathe of a flowering rush with two buds emerging. This is evidently a painted representation of an original in silver, like some of the surviving fillets,[3] with cloisonné appliqués inlaid with green, red and blue stones. A similar design appears in the tomb of the later queen Mer-es-ankh III, where the spathes emerge vertically from the diadem: the bow-tie at the back has also been transformed into a pair of papyrus umbels, while the knot has become a circular boss set between them, as almost invariably was the pattern for all practical jewels.[4]

A more stylized version of such a design appears in the second crown of the Princess Khnumet, where the diadem has become a continuous linkage of the appliqués seen on the fillet of Nofret with

Pl. 32

Pl. 18

Cf. Pl. 83

Pl. 27

21 Roundel from furniture
of Queen Hetep-her-es

the upright spathe-elements in the example worn by Mer-es-ankh III. The rosettes in all examples are probably greatly simplified versions of a roundel, consisting of a central boss with four so-called lily flowers radiating to the four points and a 'lily'-bud set between. A princess of the Fourth Dynasty had a gold fillet set with one such

Pl. 4 roundel, alternating with two papyrus-umbel bow-knots having a
Pl. 16 pair of ibises resting on them. Similar motifs appear on gilded copper head-bands at Boston and Leipzig.

Pl. 39   The crown of the Princess Sit-Hathor-Yunet from Lahun shows a restrained interpretation of the same theme. The fillet is a perfectly plain gold band to which fifteen inlaid roundels have been rivetted. The double papyrus-umbel bow-knot at the rear has become a single umbel but made in the round as a support for a flickering sheet-gold plume. The tapes at the rear have also become a pair of sheet-gold streamers hinged to one of the roundels, and are supplemented by a pair of such streamers hanging from each side. The addition of an inlaid uraeus worked *à jour* exalts this essentially plebeian headgear into a royal crown.

Other examples of the circlet designed as a crown have survived from subsequent periods. The tomb of the three queens of Tuthmosis

Pl. 61 III has yielded to date one such specimen in which the uraeus or vulture
Cf. Pl. 60 of heiress consorts has been replaced by the gazelle-head insignia of secondary queens. The circlet, which was the only crown placed over the head of Tut-ankh-amun within his coffin, has carried stylization

Pl. 123 a stage further with the narrow band bearing roundels reduced to mere carnelian bosses, and uraei attached to the side-streamers. The last variation on this design of jewel to have survived is the chaplet belonging to an infant daughter of Queen Twosre in which the fillet

Pl. 131 has been attenuated to a narrow ribbon carrying six large composite flowers in purple gold instead of simple roundels. From this it is but a short step to the crown of roses so characteristic of the Isis cult in Roman times.[5]

In the New Kingdom the boatman's circlet fell from favour as the head ornament of private persons and was replaced by the fillet,

121, 122   Ear-rings and ear-studs of Tut-ankh-amun, from Thebes ▷

123 Detail of the diadem of Tut-ankh-amun, from Thebes

124 Gold statuette of Amenophis III
from the tomb of Tut-ankh-amun,
from Thebes

apparently a band of linen, papyrus or palm-leaf secured by tapes at the rear and sewn with leaves and flower petals. These are shown, in the contemporary tomb paintings, being handed to guests together with the floral collars.[6] Doubtless more permanent versions were made in bead-work, faience or metalwork; but if so, none has survived. The only proof of their existence is the cast left in the hardened resin-soaked bandages still adhering to the despoiled mummy of Queen Meryt-amun of the early Eighteenth Dynasty, who evidently was buried wearing one or more of these fillets in bead-work instead of the boatman's circlet, or perhaps in addition to it.[7]

Another means of decorating the hair was provided by the wig ornaments that are shown on the monuments in the Early Middle Kingdom, and actual examples of which were found in the burials of Seneb-tisi and the Princess Sit-Hathor-Yunet. The first of these had ninety-eight rosettes of beaten sheet-gold interspersed at regular intervals with the tresses of her hair or wig. The princess had a great quantity of short gold tubes of two sizes which could be threaded on her braided locks in a chequer pattern so as to give the appearance of a complete gold reticulation covering the wig. Similar hair tubes were found in the treasure of Dahshur.

Pl. 23

Pls. 6, 39

A more elaborate and opulent development of these wig ornaments is found in the Eighteenth Dynasty, where the treasure of the queens of Tuthmosis III yielded the elements of at least two head-covers consisting of inlaid gold rosettes, graduated in size, strung between vertical ribs of small gold tubular beads. The complete example has a chased golden crown-plate at its summit from which falls this scintillating cascade of inlaid gold elements.

Pl. 62

Among the hair ornaments are perhaps to be included the *nekhau*, or amuletic pendant in the form of a fish, which was evidently attached to the side-lock of children, perhaps as a protection against drowning.[8] The *nekhau* was usually made of green stone; and a famous Egyptian tale tells of the consternation that was caused when the turquoise fish pendant of one of the young maidens who were rowing King Sneferu on his pleasure-lake fell into the water.[9] Several

22 Girl with fish pendant

Pls. 77, 78   such hair ornaments have survived in turquoise and gold besides other materials.

     Another hair jewel used only by children was a hair-ring or clasp for keeping the youthful side-lock in order. These must have been in fashion from the earliest times but it is only in the New Kingdom that they are represented in detail, and become increasingly elaborate as the age wears on. The sons of Ramesses III, for instance, are shown in their tomb-paintings as wearing one or more decorative slides to their side-locks.[10] No hair-rings have been positively identified and a dispute exists as to whether certain penannular gold ornaments are rings for the hair or ears (see below). It seems to the writer that the

Pl. 132   Ramessid hair-clasps take the form of small bracelets, which would provide the most convenient way of confining a thick and braided lock of hair.[11]

     The ear-ring was unknown in Egypt during the Old and Middle Kingdoms; but it comes into general use at the end of the Second Intermediate Period, probably as a result of a general dissemination of foreign ideas stimulated by the Hyksos domination, since ear-rings had been known in Asia for at least a thousand years earlier, as jewellery from the royal cemetery at Ur reveals.[12] The first notable ex-

Pl. 48   ample found in Egypt is a pair, each made of four penannular ribbed tubes soldered together, which comes from a woman's burial at Western Thebes that may be dated to the last years of the Seventeenth Dynasty.[13] Such rings were worn through holes of large diameter perforated in the ear-lobes, judging by the size of that portion of the jewel which was to be inserted. So unlikely has it seemed to some Egyptologists that these rings could be worn in the ear, that examples have been described as hair-rings; and it has been assumed that the tresses they were designed to keep in place were introduced into the gap in the ring almost hair by hair until the ring was packed tight.[14] Experiment by the writer, however, has shown that the springy nature of living hair prevents penannular rings from staying in place; and no such ornaments can be seen in representations of women's coiffures on the monuments, however detailed they may be. An

even larger, semi-circular, hole must have been made for the penannular rings made in red jasper that have been retrieved in such quantity
from burial-grounds. A number of these stone ear-rings have per- Pl. 68
forations on their periphery to take pendants. Heavy rings in thick
gold or bronze have a similar exceptionally narrow gap in which to Pl. 131
insert the ear-lobe;[15] and the problem remains of how they were
fitted to the ears. Perhaps, like their stone counterparts, they were
clipped on to the ear in infancy. The metal specimens may have been
pinched together once they had been inserted, but no such method of
closure could have been employed on the stone rings.

The most popular ear-ring during the Eighteenth Dynasty was
made of a number of hollow triangular gold hoops soldered together
and these were evidently worn by women, a pair in each ear-lobe, if
we are to judge by four examples still *in situ* on the mummy of a
woman at Turin, and the double perforations in the ears of Tuyu at *Cf.* Pl. 117
Cairo.[16] The fashion for wearing a ring in the ear was less popular
with men and was slow to be adopted. Yuya, the husband of Tuyu,
has unpierced ear-lobes, though large ear-rings for men had been in
use for at least two generations.[17] The ear-lobes of Tuthmosis III are
apparently unpierced, whereas those of his son Amenophis II have
small perforations. Mai-her-pra, Tuthmosis IV, and Tut-ankh-
amun, however, had a large hole in each ear that would have taken
the thick tubes from which their ear-ornaments were suspended. It Pls. 121, 122
has been assumed that such ear-rings were worn by boys only until
the age of puberty when they were laid aside.[18] Tomb paintings and
reliefs exist, however, showing that on occasion adult men wore Pl. 116
ear-rings.[19]

Parallel with the development of the ear-ring goes the evolution
of the ear-stud which was introduced at the Amarna Period.[20] Mushroom-shaped specimens in stone, glass, metal or faience have been Pl. 68
found in which the shank could be inserted in the hole in the ear-lobe,
leaving the circular boss, either plain or decorated, on the outside
and in the plane of the ear, not at right angles to it, as is the case with
the ear-rings. A relief of Queen Tiye shows her wearing a stud in the

23, 24 *Sweret*-beads

form of a flower, the long stem of which has been threaded through the hole in her ear-lobe.[21] Sculptures of Nefert-iti and Tiye depict them wearing large plugs or studs in their ears.[22] It is in fact at this period that the stud developed into the plug, a disk of metal or faience with a grooved edge that could be inserted into large holes in the ear-lobes. The earliest known example is the specimen believed to

Pl. 68 come from the Royal Tomb at Amarna, and now in Edinburgh, which has a heavy ornamental disk with a wide flange in place of a shank. The granular and filigree work on this specimen has a somewhat un-Egyptian appearance and the fashion for such barbaric jewels may have spread from Asia. From this point of time, however,

Pl. 134 the practice of wearing ever heavier and larger ear-plugs developed steadily in Egypt until by the Twenty-first Dynasty the women of the ruling house were wearing, in addition to ear-rings, plugs of such a size that their ear-lobes were distended to mere stringy loops of flesh, as their mummies plainly reveal.[23] Subsequent dynasties, however, show a less extreme form of fashionable mutilation, though it is true that we lack the mummies of the royal women from which to draw a proper comparison.

In contrast to such barbarities, the Egyptians did not perforate the septum or wings of the nose for the insertion of a ring, though such an ornament was in use in Asia and Nubia. A statuette, formerly

Pl. 147 in the Amherst Collection, shows a Nubian woman or godling, with her brood of children represented as apes, each wearing a silver nose-ring. A burial of the tenth century BC, excavated at Abydos, yielded a nose-ring in position on the body of a woman; but this is an isolated case and she may well have been a foreigner.[24]

The ornaments for the neck are developments of the charm strung upon a cord. At one extreme they become pectorals; at the other, collars. The pebble polished, perforated, and threaded on a string of leather or linen is one of the commonest amulets of pre-historic times; and this primitive jewel survived in the barrel-shaped carnelian *sweret*-bead, usually flanked by a green cylindrical or ball

Cf. Pl. 21 bead which the texts specify should be hung around the neck or on the breast of the deceased.[25] Sometimes a large number of such beads are mentioned, so that the pendant has in effect become a necklace. A string of shell, stone or faience beads is found in even the poorest of burials; and a number of such necklaces connected by spacer elements becomes the collar.

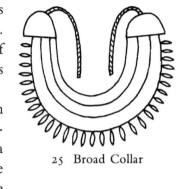

25   Broad Collar

The collar in ancient Egypt is so universal that it is virtually an item of dress. The most popular version is the Broad Collar, composed of cylindrical beads or tubes strung vertically in rows in a semi-circular or penannular shape and terminating in two lunate end-pieces, and a lowermost row of drop beads. Such collars are found painted on statues and reliefs from the Early Old Kingdom, but have rarely been recovered intact, though a notable gold and faience example of Sixth Dynasty date is at Boston. A version of the Broad Collar known as the 'Collar of the Falcon', with terminals in the form of falcon heads, is often found painted on coffins and in funerary contexts.[26] A number of actual examples have survived in various materials: faience, metal and stone. More elaborate versions substitute beads fashioned as hieroglyphs for the simple tubes of the main body of the collar.

Pl. 18

Pl. 19

26   Falcon Collar

The coffin pictures[27] of the Middle Kingdom also acquaint us with the 'Collar of Green Stone', the 'Collar of Lapis Lazuli', and the 'Collar of Gold', the 'Collar of Silver' and the 'Collar of Electrum', referring to the kind of beads used in their composition. But there are also other funerary collars, apparently cut out of sheet-gold and chased in the form of birds with wings outspread and curving up into a semi-circular shape. Such collars are described as of the god Horus, in the form of a falcon; of the goddess Nekhebet, in the form of a vulture; of the goddess Edjo, in the form of a vulture, but with a cobra's head; and of the goddesses Edjo and Nekhebet with two bodies or heads. Actual examples are very rare, probably because they were proper only to royal burials. The few that do survive have been found on the bodies of Pharaohs. Tut-ankh-amun, for instance was covered with sets of such collars not only in sheet-gold but also in flexible cloisonné-work of great elaboration.[28]

27   Collar of Edjo and Nekhebet

28 Wife of Mereruka
wearing a *menkhet*

Pl. 15

29, 30 Pendants

All such collars were designed to be worn with a *menkhet*, a counterpoise which hung down the back of the neck and balanced some of the weight of the collar in front. Such counterpoises are pictured on the monuments, but few examples worn in life with a Broad Collar appear to have survived, although funerary versions do exist, notably those in both plain sheet-gold and cloisonné-work which were inserted in the wrappings of Tut-ankh-amun.[29]

With the Eighteenth Dynasty a new type of collar, a bead version of a garland of flowers and leaves, makes its appearance. In such collars the terminals are usually in the form of lotus flowers and buds. The natural garlands were made by sewing rows of leaves, flower-petals, berries and fruits, interspersed with faience beads, onto several sheets of papyrus and securing the ends by tapes. This type of floral collar persisted even as a funerary adjunct, sometimes appearing with falcon-head terminals on the coffins of all subsequent periods.

A special kind of necklace is the choker, closely hugging the column of the neck just below the chin; this is a narrow band of bead-work, with spacers at intervals, worn by women during the Old Kingdom. It was evidently secured at the back with tie strings, if we are to judge from the coffin pictures of the Middle Kingdom; by then it had ceased to be fashionable, though it is still represented in the Late Period on figures of goddesses wearing archaic dress.

The simple jewel in the form of a single pendant or amulet, such as the *sweret*-bead hanging from a cord around the neck, developed on different lines from the necklaces into the pectoral. In the Old Kingdom such pendants occur sporadically, being attached to a cord strung at intervals with supplementary beads, and have the appearance of shells, or shell-forms made in other materials.[30] A common pendant shown on the monuments of the Old Kingdom as the regalia of palace officials, is the fetish of the goddess Bat, which later was transformed into the sistrum of the cognate deity Hathor.[31] This jewel is in the form of the cow-eared face of a woman wearing in-curving horns on her head and a trapezoidal panel of beads falling below her chin. The pendant is frequently combined with a girdle knot. The figure of Bat sometimes appears as a decorative element in the pectoral ornaments of the jewellery of the Old and Middle Kingdoms, after which she loses her identity to the great goddess Hathor.

Some representations of the Broad Collar during the Old King-dom show a bead panel hanging from the centre of the lower edge as a pectoral. This panel can also be attached to the collar by straps; or can be independent of it, hanging from the neck by straps that pass over or under the Broad Collar. Sometimes it takes a trapezoidal shape, probably inspired by a lotus-flower which is occasionally worn hanging down from the neck. The lower border of such pectorals is finished as a row of drop beads, and its straps end in falcon-head terminals.

31 Pendant with Bat insignia, tomb of Khufu-khaf

32 Boatmen with lotus flower pectorals

During the Middle Kingdom, both types of pectoral underwent a rapid development. Large trimmed pearl-shells were worn as pendants, particularly in Nubia where they were popular until very recently.[32] They were frequently inscribed with the protective name of the reigning Pharaoh. More sophisticated versions made in precious metals or cloisonné-work have survived from the period and each of the princesses buried at Dahshur appears to have had at least one pendant of this type in her parure. The trapezoidal pectoral is also inscribed with the prophylactic name of the Pharaoh, and in the royal jewels is transformed into the kiosk-shaped primeval shrine which acts as a frame for the king's cartouche supported by heraldic devices, whether in the form of plants or animals. If the name

33 Daughter of Khufu-khaf

Pls. 45, 79

Pls. 25, 26, 80, 81

Pls. 99, 100, 101

Pl. 56

Pls. 93, 96, 98, 140

Pl. 67

Pl. 35

Pl. 45

Pl. 36

is absent, the royal attributes are represented in symbolic form.[33] Such pectorals were worn in life on simple bead necklaces, though other contemporary examples have straps of beadwork. Later specimens, such as those belonging to Tut-ankh-amun, are very elaborate with intricate straps and counterpoises.

The importance of the pectoral ornament increases with the rise in popularity of the scarab amulet (see p. 160 below). By the beginning of the New Kingdom a large image of this beetle carved in a green stone had replaced other stone pendants worn on the breast of the deceased. Such 'heart-scarabs', inscribed with magical texts which insured the wearer against self-condemnation at the Last Judgment, are common thereafter and are incorporated as a central element in the design of the shrine-shaped pectorals. But all such scarab pectorals are restricted to funerary use.

The jewel worn over the hips by women was the girdle, the chief function of which was amuletic (see p. 16 above). Girdles are not represented in the Old Kingdom when women, even servant-girls as distinct from children, are not represented in the nude. In the Middle Kingdom, concubine figures in faience, wood, clay and other materials are sometimes shown as wearing cowrie-shell girdles.[34] In the New Kingdom there are many pictures of nude handmaidens and young girls clearly wearing the girdle about their hips: sometimes it is shown as though worn outside the gown.[35]

One of the earliest complete examples has been retrieved from the deposit of Sit-Hathor-Yunet. The large beads are in the form of hollow gold cowrie-shells strung on two cords with acacia-seed beads of gold, green felspar and carnelian spaced between. The princesses buried at Dahshur also had cowrie-shell girdles, one of slightly different pattern; and similar girdles in gold and silver have been found in other burial-grounds of the Middle Kingdom.[36] Towards the end of her life, Sit-Hathor-Yunet acquired another girdle of different design with the large beads in the form of double leopard heads, and the spacer-beads of identical shape but on a smaller scale. The two strings were threaded with amethyst ball beads.

133   Bracelets of the High Priest Pi-nudjem II, from Thebes ▷

134   Ear-plugs of Ramesses XI, from Abydos ▷

135 Bracelets of Psusennes I, from Tanis

141 Pendant of Osorkon II

142   *Ba*-bird pendant, upper side, from Saqqara

143   *Ba*-bird pendant, under side, from Saqqara

Another of the Dahshur girdles was of a similar design which, however, had a very brief fashion, being replaced before the New Kingdom by girdles of less massive appearance with modest spacer-beads Pl. 48
of semi-circular shape separated by small ring or barrel beads. In one
example belonging to a queen of Tuthmosis III, the spacers are in the Pl. 63
form of the fish amulet.

Belts as distinct from girdles were worn by men to support their Pl. 132
kilts around the waist; but a development of the woman's girdle is
the belt worn by one or more of the queens of Tuthmosis III. This Pl. 63
was composed of seven rows of acacia-seed beads, similar to the
specimens in Sit-Hathor-Yunet's earlier girdle, in gold, carnelian,
turquoise, and probably blue faience or glass. The gold beads are
soldered together to make spacer-bars and two plain bars form the
clasp. Elements of three belts of different lengths have survived, but
only enough beads have been secured by the Metropolitan Museum
to make one complete example. Such pieces of women's costume
jewellery are unknown from any other source and are not represented
on the monuments: they probably reflect a foreign fashion adapted
by an Egyptian jeweller.

ORNAMENTS OF THE LIMBS

The ornaments of the arm, which were worn by both sexes, comprise
armlets for the upper arm and bracelets for the wrists. They could be
either flexible or rigid, depending upon whether their prototype
was a string of beads or a section of elephant tusk, a type of bangle
which is still in fashion today in various parts of Africa. In the Old
and Middle Kingdoms, only bracelets were worn: armlets do not
make their appearance on the monuments until the beginning of the
New Kingdom.[37] Nevertheless, it is probable that single strings of
beads were sometimes worn above the elbow, as was found to be
the case when the mummy of Princess Ashyet of the Eleventh
Dynasty came to be unwrapped.[38]

The rigid armlets are copies of shell or ivory prototypes. The
earliest known example in gold dates to the Archaic Period, but the Pl. 13

Pl. 3 silver bracelets of Queen Hetep-her-es are of the same design, though inlaid with coloured stones. Such bracelets in graduated sets

Pl. 115 were worn only by women on the forearms. They went out of fashion during the later Fourth Dynasty. The simple ring bangle, square in cross section, was originally of ivory, but in time, versions in metal and faience were also made.[39] During the Eighteenth Dynasty they appear to have been worn in pairs on the upper arm,

Pl. 116 particularly during the period from Amenophis II to Amenophis III.

Pl. 58 A metal version of what looks like an ivory bracelet is found in the reign of the latter king worn on the wrist of one arm only,[40] whereas in the reign of his son Akhenaten, an example is worn on each wrist.[41]

The jewellery from the tomb of King Djer at Abydos shows that flexible bead bracelets were in use by the First Dynasty, and the future development lay only in the use of spacer-beads and an increase in the number of strings of beads that could be incorporated into such jewels by lengthening the spacer-bars. Methods of fastening the ends of the band together were also devised as an improvement on

Pl. 14 the mere knotting of tie-strings which was apparently the original means if we are to trust the coffin pictures of the Middle Kingdom.

Fig. 34 The Dahshur and Lahun bracelets had a detachable inlaid member which was part of the decorative pattern and could be slid into position

Pl. 40 on grooved bars forming the terminal spacers of the beadwork.

An elaboration of the simple string of beads worn on the upper arm, as for instance by Princess Ashyet, is the so-called motto-clasp favoured by the royal women of the next dynasty. These are inlaid jewels composed of glyphs and symbols forming a name, motto, or good wish; and were fastened to the upper arm with a cord or string of small gold beads.[42] Associated with them are other single strings of beads incorporating figures of recumbent lions, which were ap-

Pls. 34, 44 parently worn by the princesses as bracelets.[43] By the time of King Kamose of the Seventeenth Dynasty such jewels had become armlets. He had a pair of lions flanking the name of his brother Amosis; they had originally been tied by a stout cord around his right arm, though they were found loose in the debris in his coffin.[44] The motto-clasp

34 Anklet fastening

had thus become combined with the lion figurines, and the integra-
tion of the two types of bracelet is found in the complete gold armlet
belonging to Kamose's mother, Queen Ah-hotpe, who in life certainly wore it above her elbow. Similar feline animals, such as cats
and sphinxes made in gold or hardstones, are incorporated in the
jewellery dated to the centuries following the fall of the Twelfth
Dynasty and are still to be seen in the armlets of the queens of Tuthmosis III.

Pls. 51, 52

Pl. 84

The flexible wristlets and the rigid bangles combine their functions in the hinged bracelets which also appear at the beginning of the
New Kingdom, when two half-cylinders of metal are hinged together at both edges, one hinge having a retractable pin to allow the
encircling band to be opened.[45] Simple plain bracelets of gold in this
design were supplied for the queens of Tuthmosis III; but other
bracelets in the parure were more elaborate, with inlays of ribbed
carnelian, felspar and glass cemented in position, being in fact rigid
versions of the bead-and-spacer bracelets of the Middle Kingdom.

Pl. 54

Pl. 85

Pl. 64

As the New Kingdom progressed, even more opulent arm
ornaments were made in this design; and the carnelian and sard
plaques of Amenophis III, the massive bracelets and armlets found on
the limbs of Tut-ankh-amun, and the gold bracelets of Ramesses II
from the Tell Basta hoard are all in the same tradition. So are the silver
pair found in the burial of Queen Twosre's daughter, though their
flimsy construction may owe much to the probability that they were
destined only for funerary use.

Pls. 87–89, 110, 112,
129

The ornaments of the legs, the anklets, are indistinguishable in
design and manufacture from those of the arms. In the coffin pictures
they are identical; and both in actuality and on the monuments they
were made *en suite*. Generally, however, the anklets are rather less
deep than the bracelets, though not, for instance, in the case of the
jewellery worn by a daughter of Djehuti-hotpe at Deir el-Bersha.
They are shown as worn by women only until the early Ramessid
period.[47] As it is physically impossible to pass a rigid ring over the
instep so as to make it fit snugly around the lower leg, anklets were at

35   Bracelet

36   Anklet

Fig. 37

Pl. 137

first of flexible beadwork secured with ties or clasps. Later, they too were made solid and hinged in two halves, so that it is difficult to distinguish them from bracelets.[48] One such specimen, found on the body of Tut-ankh-amun, has been identified as a bracelet, though it was found in the region of the King's legs.[49] It is probable that all such leg ornaments were worn just above the ankle.

Pls. 12, 36

A peculiarity of women's anklets in the Middle Kingdom is the bird-claw pendant worn on a string or double string of beads. Some of these pendants are very elaborate; the specimens belonging to the Princess Khnumet found at Dahshur were of gold work, with an imbricated pattern in cloisonné-work. Usually one claw only was worn over the outer ankle-bone, but anklets exist where several claws are spaced at intervals on the same string of beads.

Towards the end of the Old Kingdom there came into fashion a novel type of seal, to which archaeologists have given the description 'button seal' from the appearance of the majority of such objects. They are usually made of glazed steatite, but may be carved from other substances. They were soon ousted from favour by the scarab, however, which was partly an amulet and partly a signet. Many thousands of scarabs were thenceforward to be made in Egypt, mostly in glazed steatite but also in other materials, and have become the characteristic product of ancient Egypt and of modern forgers.

Essentially they are objects of cabochon shape, pierced through their greater diameter by a thread-hole, the convexity being carved more or less realistically as a scarab beetle, and the base usually incised with an inscription. The first scarabs may have been worn like a bead on a string; but the custom soon arose of tying them on the fingers by a thread. In more permanent examples, the thread was replaced by gold wire; and at that point the signet ring had been invented. The

37 Dancer from Qau

Pl. 46

finds at Dahshur and Lahun yielded nearly three dozen scarabs in cloisonné-work and precious stones inscribed with the names of the princesses or contemporary Pharaohs, as well as decorative devices. About a third of them are strung on gold wire rings with their ends coiled to imitate linen thread.

During the Second Intermediate Period the finger ring underwent a full mechanical development,[51] the wire being thickened into
a rod of hoop shape with knopped ends, around which the thinner
suspensory wire could be wrapped. The next stage was to flatten the
knops and perforate them, in order to take a thick wire rivet on which
the scarab could turn. Another method was to draw out the ends of a
length of thick wire bent into a ring and to insert them from opposite
ends of the hole in the scarab, coiling the emergent lengths onto the   Pl. 69
body of the ring. At the same time the scarab itself was mounted in a
gold or silver funda with tubes to take the rivet or wires. The last   Pl. 136
stage in the development was to cast the ring and a non-swivelling
scarab-shaped bezel in one piece, and such massive metal signet rings   Pls. 69, 70
are characteristic of the Amarna Period, when lighter versions in
faience were also made, probably for distribution as favours on the
occasion of festivals and Court functions. Different ways of making
metal finger-rings, however, were employed at the same time; but
the only change that the finger-ring underwent in post-Amarna
times was a tendency for the bezel to be isolated from the mass of the
ring and to assume more the appearance of an inscribed plate attached
to a hoop.[52]

Other amulets, such as the *wedjet*-eye, in hard stones, may take
the place of the scarab in finger-rings worn for decorative or protective   Pls. 69, 136
purposes. The ring with an inscribed bezel acting as a signet appears
to be an Egyptian invention, the development of which can be traced.
It is worthy of note, however, that decorative types of finger-rings,
fully evolved, appear in the Dahshur treasure,[53] and since their bezels
are ornamented with granular designs, it is probable that the finger-
ring, as distinct from the signet, was in origin an Asiatic import.

There are several jewels which, although represented on the
monuments, have not been found in actuality. Thus queen-mothers
and principal queens are shown on state occasions wearing an elaborate ornament on their hair or wigs in the form of the feathered   Pl. 127
skin of a vulture, its head thrust forward over the brow, the body
fitting the skull like a cap, its tail descending over the occiput, and

Pl. 62 each wing and leg falling on each side of the head behind the ear. The wig-cover at New York, however, gives us more than a hint of how such jewels were made in reality. They must have been composed of plates of gold cloisonné-work, threaded together to form a flexible headgear of great magnificence and no little weight.

Pl. 105 There are also stoles in bead-work, of which only one possible example has survived from the tomb of Tut-ankh-amun. Certain garments peculiar to the king, such as the imbricated corselets and Pl. 132 the apron hanging from the belt, though made in gold cloisonné-work, are to be regarded more as items of dress than as jewels. Again, the only specimens known belong to Tut-ankh-amun.[54] In the same category of clothing are to be placed the belts made of bead-work, Pl. 9 sometimes in the funerary versions having an apron of long bead pendants. An exception, however, is perhaps to be made of the belt of Prince Ptah-Shepses of the Fifth Dynasty, which is more the work of the jeweller than the tailor.[55]

Pl. 24 The thin ribbons, presumably of gold in the wealthiest examples, which bound the bouffant coiffures or wigs of women in the Middle Kingdom and Early New Kingdom, have not been found intact; and the bobbins with carnelian bosses[56] around which the ends of Pls. 24, 32 the two large pendent wings of these same wigs were wound have not been identified. Conversely, a curious amuletic pendant in the form of a tubular case, usually decorated in various ways, and Pl. 46 generally hollow though sometimes solid, has never satisfactorily been explained, though it is often found in the graves of women during the Middle Kingdom,[57] and even as late as the reign of Tuthmosis III.

Epilogue

For reasons which we have already emphasized, the mass of Pharaonic jewellery that has eluded the depredations of time and man is relatively small and hardly representative of the craft throughout its long history in Ancient Egypt. But although the small extent of this random sampling has allowed it to be studied fairly intensively, a great number of questions still await answers, particularly in regard to ancient techniques and designs. The technical examination of Egyptian jewellery by modern craftsmen has suffered from too ready an assumption that the ancient jewellers used most of the materials, tools and processes available today, when it is clear that such is not the case. Before any further progress can be made along this line of research, museum authorities will have to sanction the use of more scientific means of examining ancient jewellery; and the microscope, X-rays and the spectroscope will have to be pressed into service much more than they have been used in the past. At the moment, no accurate analyses of many ancient materials, and particularly of their trace elements have been recorded. Without fuller and more accurate data it is idle to speculate on the nature of ancient technical processes, the trade routes by which they were disseminated and the cultural contacts that they demonstrate.

The studies by Winlock and others have shown what a valuable contribution stylistic analysis can make to the recovery of the forms and appearance of ancient jewellery: but more remains to be done in this field of design. Lastly, in an age of increased awareness of the importance of 'conservation', it should not need to be stressed that when they were first displayed in all their splendour, the jewels of the Pharaohs did not exhibit that tarnish and damage which are all too often their portion today.

Chronological Table

Note: All dates are BC. Only the names of the kings or queens mentioned in the text are given their place in this table.

Archaic Period c.3100–2686

Dynasty I c.3100............................. Djer c.3045–3020
Dynasty II c.2890............ Kha-sekhem-wy c.2704–2686

Old Kingdom c.2686–2160

Dynasty III c.2686............... Sekhem-khet c.2642–2638
Dynasty IV c.2613............ Queen Hetep-her-es fl. c.2600
Dynasty V c.2494........................ Sahu-re c.2483–2469
.... Nefer-ir-ka-re c.2469–2460
Dynasty VI c.2345 ....
Dynasties VII–VIII c.2181–2160 ....

First Intermediate Period c.2160–2040

Dynasties IX–X ....
Dynasty XI (part) ....

Middle Kingdom c.2040–1633

Dynasty XI (part) c.2040............ Queen Nofru fl. c.2020
Dynasty XII 1991............... Ammenemes II 1929–1895
.... Sesostris II 1897–1878
....Sesotris III 1878–1843
.... Ammenemes III 1842–1797
Dynasty XIII 1786–1633...

Second Intermediate Period c.1633–1559

Dynasty XIV c.1786–1600 ....
Dynasties XV, XVI c. 1674–1559...........................
(Hyksos Kings) ....
Dynasty XVII c. 1650–1559 ....
(Theban Kings).................Sobek-em-saf II fl. c. 1630
.... Nub-kheper-re Intef fl. c.1600
.... Kamose c.1562–1559
.... Queen Ah-hotpe c.1580–1540

New Kingdom 1559–1085

Dynasty XVIII 1559........................Amosis 1559–1531
....Tuthmosis III 1490–1436
.... Amenophis III 1405–1367
....Akhenaten 1378–1362
.... Tut-ankh-amun 1362–1353
Dynasty XIX 1320......................Ramesses II 1304–1237
.... Sethos II c.1223–1218
.... Queen Twosre c. 1223–1200
Dynasty XX 1200......................Ramesses III 1198–1166
.... Ramesses IX 1140–1121

Tanites 1085–945

Dynasty XXI...................... Psusennes I c.1070–1052
.... Amenophthis c.1052–1003

Libyans 945–751

Dynasties XXII–XXIV.............. Osorkon II c.860–832

Late Period 751–332

Dynasties XXV–XXXI ....
(Kushites, Saites, Persians) ....

Ptolemies 332–30

144 'Horses' ring of Ramesses II, from Saqqara

145 Pectoral of Ramesses II, from Saqqara

146 Miniature Broad Collar
from a Late Period statue

147 Statuette of a Nubian woman
with attendant apes wearing nose-rings

148 Wall-painting of the weighing of gold, Western Thebes

152   Small jewel casket of Princess Sit-Hathor-Yunet, from Lahun

153   Marquetry casket from the tomb of Tut-ankh-amun at Thebes

154   View into the Treasury of the tomb of Tut-ankh-amun,
guarded by the Anubis pylon ▷

151 Bust of Ammenemes III, from Medinet el-Fayum

150   Bust of Ramesses II, from Tanis

149 Women with collars, detail of a relief of Nefer-seshem-Psamtik, from Memphis

155, 156 Top and side view of cartouche-shaped box from the tomb of Tut-ankh-amun at Thebes

1 Bracelets, from the cenotaph (?) of King Djer at Abydos. First Dynasty, *c.* 3020 BC. In the Cairo Museum.

In 1901 Flinders Petrie continued his re-excavation of the ravaged archaic sites at Abydos, where the tombs or cenotaphs of the first Pharaohs had been made. He found in a crevice in the brick-work of the complex of Djer, the third king of the First Dynasty, the wrapped forearm of a woman of the royal household. This had evidently been thrust out of sight by one of the officials who cleared up the plundered tomb in the reign of Amenophis III when it was wrongly identified as the resting-place of Osiris, the great god of Abydos. Petrie found the bracelets held in position by the wrappings and was thus able to recover their original order of stringing. They are shown in the plate in the sequence in which they were found, the top specimen being nearest the wrist.

Top row: Bracelet (now in two halves) gold, lapis lazuli and turquoise. L. (of each part) 3·7 and 2·2 cm. Cat. No. 52011.

The two parts when found were joined by strings of hair (perhaps from giraffe-tails) and gold wires of equal thickness plaited together. The front half has as its central feature a hollow gold rosette, made with great skill in imitation of a half-opened flower. It is pierced with holes through which run three threads carrying turquoise beads, irregular in shape but highly polished, alternating with gold ball beads and ring beads soldered in threes to form spacers. Both strings are caught at each extremity by a single lapis lazuli ball bead and a hollow gold ball bead. The rear half inverses the order at the ends so that a lapis lazuli follows a gold bead. The fastening was by means of a loop and gold ball button which, however, are not shown on the plate.

Second row: Bracelet, gold and turquoise. L. 15·6 cm. Cat. No. 52008. This, the most celebrated of the quartet, consists of thirteen gold and fourteen turquoise graduated plaques in the form of the king's *serekh* surmounted by a falcon. The *serekh* was a representation of the facade and ground-plan of the king's palace. The king's name, as the incarnation of the distant sky-god Horus, is usually inscribed within the *serekh*. Here it is rendered as Djer. The gold *serekhs* appear to have been formed by casting the shape in an open mould and afterwards tooling the cast. The end-pieces were made by flattening hollow gold cones and soldering an oval plate, pierced with two holes, over the open end. All elements are perforated with holes so as to thread on two separate strings which are twisted to become one tie-cord where they emerge from the hole at the tip of each end-piece.

Third row: Bracelet, gold, amethyst and turquoise. L. 15 cm. Cat. No. 52010.

This is the most original bracelet in the group, its design being based upon beads of hour-glass shape, probably representing the insect of the goddess Neith (*cf.* Plate 5). They are strung in four vertical groups of three, alternating with a larger horizontal example. Each vertical group consists of two gold beads flanking a central amethyst bead (in one place the amethyst is replaced by a dark brown stone). Each horizontal group consists of two lozenge-shaped turquoise beads having gold caps and being joined by a gold bi-conal connector. There are three such beads graduated in size so that the largest is in the middle, and each is separated from the vertical group by a turquoise ball bead. The bracelet was strung on two thick hairs threaded through the horizontal beads and woven around the central groove in each vertical hour-glass bead. These were held in position by whipping the hairs on either side with fine gold wire.

Bottom row: Bracelet, gold, lapis lazuli and turquoise. L. 13 cm. Cat. No. 52009.

This bracelet is similar in design to the one in the top row, consisting of three rows of beads caught at four points by single large ball beads. The various elements are of two main types. The first is a barrel bead in gold made by winding a gold wire which is thinner at its extremities around a suitable mandrel. A dark lapis lazuli bead is carved with ribs to imitate the same shape. The second is a ball bead of turquoise or hollow gold, the latter originally soldered in groups of three to form spacers with the exception of six single large specimens. The beads are threaded in graduated groups so that the largest comes at the middle of the string. A double loop-and-button fastening was provided at both ends of this bracelet.

Petrie's words which he penned on first discovering these bracelets *in situ* are still worth quoting: 'Here, at the crystallizing point of Egyptian art, we see the unlimited variety and fertility of design. Excepting the plain gold balls, there is not a single bead in any one bracelet which would be interchangeable with those in another bracelet. Each is of independent design, fresh and free from all convention or copying. And yet not one of these would be in place among the jewellery of the XIIth Dynasty' (*cf.* Plates 27–46).

2 Parure, gold, from a burial of First Dynasty date. In the Cairo Museum.

In 1903 G. A. Reisner excavated an archaic tomb at Nag-ed-Der in which the mass of the super-structure had collapsed, crushing the body beneath it and preserving it from the attentions of robbers who had been active in other parts of the necropolis. The deceased had originally worn a plain gold circlet around the brows and bracelets in flint, slate and copper, in addition to plain gold rings which may be among the earliest finger-rings known. Ten package-shaped gold amulets, beads in garnet and carnelian and black-and-white stone pendants were also retrieved.

Centre: Two pendants, gold. L. 4 cm. and 3·8 cm. Cat. Nos. 53824–5.

The animal on the left is a steer (Apis bull?), the horns of which are missing. From its neck hangs a pendant in the form of the 'aegis' of the goddess Bat (*cf.* Plates 26, 34). The animal on the right is an oryx with a *tyet* (girdle-tie) around its neck. Both have been made by working a thin sheet of gold by the repoussé technique, backing it with a pink cement (plaster?) and soldering it to a flat plate carrying two tubes for receiving the tie-strings of a necklace, or even a single suspensory cord.

Outer: A necklace of twenty-four gold shells. L. (of each) 1·5 cm. Cat. No. 53802.

Each hemispheroidal shell has been formed by hammering gold foil into a suitable mould and enhancing the coils by repoussé. A ring has been skilfully soldered on the outside at each extremity. Originally the beads were threaded on two strings and perhaps held in position by knotting, but of such suspension no traces remained.

3   Bracelets of Queen Hetep-her-es, silver, inlaid with carnelian, lapis lazuli and turquoise. Outer diam. 9 to 11 cm. Excavated by G. A. Reisner at Giza. IVth Dynasty. In the Museum of Fine Arts, Boston (Mass). Reg. Nos. 47.1699–1701.

The greatly decayed secondary burial of the mother of Kheops was found in the vicinity of that king's Great Pyramid on the Giza plateau in 1925, and most skillfully excavated by the Harvard-Boston Expedition. The deposit contained among other spectacular items, the remains of a gold encased wooden box carrying two removeable tapered rollers for the storage of twenty silver bracelets worn on the forearms in the manner shown in contemporary reliefs (*cf.* Plate 15). The bracelets follow the pattern of such ornaments of the Archaic Period (*cf.* Plate 13), being formed as hollow shells of thin metal but with depressions worked in them for the reception of the stone inlays cemented in position. These inlays, in which lapis lazuli has been eked out in places with painted plaster, represent schematic butterflies. Four of the bracelets in the queen's two sets have survived only in a greatly decayed condition and two such specimens presented to the Boston Museum are illustrated here.

4, 5 Parure of a woman of the royal house, excavated at Giza in the Re-wer tomb complex (shaft No. 294) by Selim Hassan in 1931. IVth Dynasty. In the Cairo Museum.

4 A circlet, gold, copper and carnelian. L. 56 cm. D. (of central rosette) 7·8 cm.
The simple gold fillet found on a burial of the Archaic Period and referred to in the note on Plate 2 above, has here assumed the sophisticated form common in the Old Kingdom (*cf.* Plate 16). The thin strip of gold foil, 3·8 cm. wide, has been strengthened by a backing of copper sheet covered with gold leaf. The band is not continuous but is perforated at each end to take the tie-cord, which would hang as a bow-knot behind. The decoration, with strong echoes of the marsh-flora familiar to the boatman, consists of two flower shapes. The central rosette has a chased design of four flowering rush forms united about a central carnelian boss. The other two identical roundels each comprise two opposed papyrus umbels about a central, carnelain-set, boss with two ibises nesting on their upper edges.

5 A collar, gold, L. (of each bead) 2·7 cm. D. *c.* 16 cm.
In addition to the circlet shown in Plate 4, the body of the woman found by Selim Hassan at Giza was adorned with bracelets of gold and copper at the wrists and ankles and wore a necklace of gold and faience beads strung on gold wire with gold clasps at the ends. Its unique adornment, however, was the collar illustrated here which consists of fifty hollow gold beads in the form of the beetle *Agrypnus notodonta Latr.*, made by working thin sheet into a stone or wooden mould and soldering a ring at the head end. The beetles are strung on two wires, one threading the head-rings and the other running through perforations in the shells near the junction of the elytra with the prothorax, to form a semi-flexible circlet of radiating elements. The beetle in question, which may be a forerunner of the scarab (see p. 160) was sacred to Neith, a goddess of great influence in the earlier dynasties. The collar was thus not only an adornment but also an amulet placing the wearer under the protection of the chief goddess of the age.

6–9 The Egyptian Expedition of the Metropolitan Museum of Art, working at Lisht in 1907 in the vicinity of the ruined pyramid of King Ammenemes I (*c.* 1991–1962 BC), found the tomb of Seneb-tisi, a woman of the family of the Vizier Sen-wosret, which had been partly rifled and was in a greatly decayed state. The two excavators, A. C. Mace and H. E. Winlock, by patient skill, were able to recover almost completely the original form and features of the deposit, and their reconstructions of some of the funerary jewellery, now in the Metropolitan Museum, New York, are illustrated in the following four plates.
The personal jewels of Seneb-tisi had been stolen in antiquity and only traces of her wig in its crushed container were found as part of the adornments she wore during her time on earth. The jewellery illustrated here was found mostly embedded between layers of linen wrappings soaked in resin that covered the body and allowed the original order of stringing to be

determined. Some ornaments such as the circlets and rosettes, three bead necklaces, a girdle and a bracelet were worn in life, but the other jewels had served an exclusive funerary purpose.

6   Wig ornaments of the House Mistress Seneb-tisi, gold, early XIIth Dynasty. M. M. A. Reg. No. 07.227.6–7.
The rosettes, of marguerite form, each 1·1 cm. in diameter, were made by beating heavy gold sheet into a die of wood or stone. Two such moulds were employed, one with sixteen radiating divisions; the other with twelve. Eighty-five rosettes of the latter type had been pierced with two holes to take threads binding them to the tresses of the wig: the remainder have a bar of gold soldered across the back for the same purpose. These rosettes were found embedded in resin covering the head of the deceased, and have been replaced on a reconstruction of the wig or coiffure.
The circlet is of gold wire in three zones each coiled into a series of continuous loops to form a kind of expansible chain. At the back of the head the three chains were fastened by a thinner gold wire that connected the adjacent loops together. The chains were also anchored at the front, the wires being pulled straight for about 4 cm. and whipped with other lengths of wire, a heart-shaped pendant, perhaps representing a stylized flower, being formed in the process to hang over the forehead.

7   Collar, turquoise, carnelian, green faience, and gold foil filled with plaster. W. 25·5 cm., early XIIth Dynasty. Tomb of Seneb-tisi. M.M.A. Reg. No. 08.200.30.
One of the three funerary collars of Seneb-tisi of a type known as 'The Falcon' (see p. 145), from the design of its terminals, each made in the shape of the head of the bird with an eye of carnelian and markings inlaid in blue pigment. Such end-pieces were made by burnishing gold foil into suitable moulds and filling the cavity with plaster before removal. The drop beads were made by a similar means, loops being formed at each extremity before adding the plaster backing. The gold beads are mostly of plaster-filled foil; turquoise and carnelian are used for the coloured beads together with dark-green faience and probably what was originally a blue faience imitating lapis lazuli, which has now turned brown.

8   Collar, turquoise, green faience and gold foil filled with plaster. W. 25 cm., early XIIth Dynasty. Tomb of Seneb-tisi. M. M. A. Reg. No. 08.200.31.
A similar neck ornament to Plate 7, but with semi-circular end-pieces, known as a 'Broad Collar' (see p. 145). Like all such collars, it is made of tubular beads graduated in size so that the longest are in the middle of each row. In the Broad Collar here illustrated the vertical tubular beads are separated and bordered by strings of small ring beads. Both collars have the characteristic shape of such adjuncts during the XIIth Dynasty, being

U-shaped rather than quasi-circular, with the shoulder-pieces lying further apart, and rather shallower in depth than earlier examples (*cf.* Plates 18, 19, 20). It should be noted that no perforations are made in the terminals to take tie-cords (*cf.* Plate 10). Such funerary collars were merely laid on the breast of the deceased.

9 Apron, green, white, yellow, and black faience beads with some gold foil. W. 58·5 cm., early XIIth Dynasty. Tomb of Seneb-tisi. M.M.A. Reg. No. 08.200.29.

This is the most complete example to have survived of a *besau* or protective bead apron, otherwise known from the coffin pictures and representations on the monuments. Originally it was a primitive garment worn only by the Pharaoh as part of his insignia, but by the Middle Kingdom it had been appropriated for funerary use by any commoner who could afford a burial in which he would be tricked out in all the trappings of a dead king identified with Osiris. The apron consists of a beadwork belt with a buckle of wood covered with gold foil bearing the owner's name in blue pigment. At the rear hangs an imitation animal's tail in beadwork over a wooden core woven in intricate zig-zag patterns and with a gold foil ferrule at each end. From the lower edge of the belt also depend twenty-two strings of bead-work representing the heraldic plants of Upper and Lower Egypt, the flowering rush on the right and the papyrus on the left, suggesting that the deceased around whom the apron was clasped would face the rising sun, the position, in fact, in which Egyptians were buried at this period. It is almost certain that the princesses whose jewels are illustrated in the following plates (Plates 10–12, 27–46) were buried in similar aprons, of which character-istic X-shaped beads have survived. The tradition persisted into the XVIIth Dynasty at least, for the woman whose jewellery is illustrated on Plate 48 wore such an ornament, though all that was recovered was the tail in the form of a tassel of blue lentoid beads which the excavator described as a 'fly-whisk'.

10–12 Jewels from the Dahshur and Lahun Treasures. XIIth Dynasty, now in
27–46 Cairo and New York.
73–76 In 1895 the French Egyptologist J. de Morgan uncovered jewellery belong-ing to the princesses of the family of Sesostris III (*c.* 1878–1843 BC) in their tombs within the precincts of that king's pyramid, the northern brick pyra-mid, at Dahshur. Some months later he found another treasure belonging to an earlier generation of royal women in tombs in the enclosure of the ruined stone pyramid of Ammenemes II (*c.* 1929–1895 BC) at the same site. In 1914 G. Brunton, working for Flinders Petrie, excavated a similar treasure which had been buried with the Princess Sit-Hathor-Yunet in a tomb within the precincts of the brick pyramid of her father Sesostris II (1897–1878 BC)

at Lahun. All these parures, with the possible exception of that shown in Plate 10, had been used by the princesses during their lifetimes and some of them show signs of wear. They were buried with their owners in wooden caskets which, however, had decayed almost entirely by the time of their discovery (see Plate 152). These jewels are substantial pieces, made of precious and hard-wearing materials and should be compared with those of Seneb-tisi made solely for funerary use and illustrated in Plates 6–9.

10 Funerary parure of the Princess Ita-weret who was buried at Dahshur near the pyramid of her father (?) Ammenemes II. Gold, carnelian, turquoise, green faience and lapis lazuli. W. (of collar) *c.* 28 cm. In the Cairo Museum (no reg. no.).

De Morgan, at Dahshur, was fortunate in finding a considerable mass of treasure on different parts of the site; but posterity has been unfortunate in that he retrieved it in too great a haste with inadequate staff, supervision and recording. The result was that for years the Cairo Museum exhibited a rich but disordered collection of jewels and gems without any clear exposition of their original appearance. The careful work of Brunton and Winlock on the Lahun Treasure (Plates 35–40) has enabled some of the Dahshur pieces to be re-assembled into something approaching their pristine order, but much remains to be done.

The jewellery of Ita-weret illustrates the shortcomings of de Morgan's methods, or lack of them. He found the burial of this princess intact in her red granite sarcophagus, but although he did not find her jewel caskets in the tomb, or omitted to search for them, he reports that, 'at her wrists and ankles were various bracelets of gold and hardstone beads. At her neck was a large collar made of beads and ornaments of gold. It was held in position by two clasps'. His only illustration, which gives no scale or other particulars, shows the collar incorrectly strung.

Actually the Broad Collar of Ita-weret was unusual in being furnished with a *menkhet* counterpoise (see p. 146) and appears to have been one worn in life and adapted for funerary use. The semi-circular end-pieces are perforated to take the tie-strings that connect it to the counterpoise. A bracelet shown in the illustration appears to have been composed out of one of the 'various' examples from Ita-weret's ankles or wrists, but the beads have been improperly matched so that the band assumes a curved shape. It appears to have been clasped with tie-strings (*cf.* Figs. 35, 36).

11–12 Jewellery from the parure of the Princess Khnumet who probably became
29–31 a queen in later life and was buried in the vicinity of the pyramid of her father, or husband, Ammenemes II at Dahshur. Her jewels represent the products of the royal workshops during the earlier part of the XIIth Dynasty.

11 Collar, gold, inlaid with lapis lazuli, turquoise, carnelian, garnets, green felspar: size of terminals, H. 3·8 cm., W. 4·3 cm. In the Cairo Museum, Cat. Nos. 52861–2 *et. al.*

A 'Falcon Collar' tentatively reconstructed from elements recovered *en masse* by de Morgan. It comprises seven rows of pendant beads connected by strings of gold ring-beads. Four of the rows consist of three different hieroglyphs symbolizing 'Life', 'Stability' and 'Power' made of gold inlaid with coloured stones and graduated in size.

Below, part of a string of drop beads and gold ring beads from the same hoard, arbitrarily assembled.

12 *Top Row*: Parts of a pair of bracelets, gold, turquoise, lapis lazuli and carnelian. H. 3·9 cm. In the Cairo Museum, Cat. Nos. 52044–5, 52048–9.

At each extremity is a clasp consisting of a completely detachable member made of gold sliding on tongues within channels formed in two end-pieces. Each of the latter is perforated with sixteen holes to take rows of carnelian, turquoise, lapis lazuli and gold cylindrical beads strung on linen threads. The gold beads were made by slipping sections of gold tube over a tube of smaller diameter and soldering them at intervals to a base plate, so making a spacer-bar. The beads were threaded in groups to form red, green and blue bars alternating with gold spacers (*cf.* Plate 40). When the bracelet was put on the wearer, the handmaid wrapped it around the wrist of her mistress with the two grooved end-pieces opposite each other and connected them by slipping the tongued slide in between them. The design of the slide is based upon a protective *sa*-amulet inlaid in lapis lazuli, the ties being of turquoise and carnelian: at its summit is a small leopard head in gold (*cf.* Plate 36).

Middle Row: An anklet, gold inlaid with turquoise, carnelian, lapis lazuli, H. of claw pendants 2·25 cm. Cairo Museum, Cat. Nos. 52911–12 *et al.*

This jewel, as restrung, shows a pair of bird claws, having a right and left profile, strung on a thread of gold beads with a gold clasp in the form of a knot, one half of which fastens to the other by means of a T-shaped tongue sliding in a groove (*cf.* Plate 36). Each claw consists of a gold back-plate to which is soldered an upper cap chased in imitation of granular work carrying the suspension ring-bead, thus showing that the claw was intended to be hung from a single string of beads among which gold rings were included as part of the design (*cf.* Plate 36). The outer face of the body of each claw is decorated with an imbricated pattern in cloisonné-work inlaid with coloured stones.

This piece has been incorrectly restrung as a single anklet. Khnumet had only two such claws, a left and a right example, among the material retrieved by de Morgan; and it is therefore clear that each anklet should consist of a single claw falling over the outer ankle bone and suspended from a string of beads encircling the leg. It is also probable that each string consisted of gold, carnelian, lapis lazuli and turquoise beads strung in groups to repeat the colours of the inlays on the claws themselves.

Bottom Row: Necklace of carnelian, turquoise and lapis lazuli *ankh*-signs, with a gold *ankh*-'clasp'. H. of clasp 1·9 cm. Cairo Museum, Cat. Nos. 53012–3, 52916.

This necklace, exhibited upside down and curving in the opposite direction to which it should take, is also reconstructed and is incomplete. The 'clasp' is made of gold with two bars, each perforated with three holes, sliding on tongues forming the sides of a trapezoid framing the *ankh*. Each stone *ankh* is made in two parts, the upper loop and cross-bar, and the lower tongue. In its original form, the *ankhs* were kept in position by matching ring beads packed on the threads that passed through the upper and lower perforated lugs on each complete sign. A medial thread passed up a hole drilled the length of each tongue into a transverse hole in the cross-bar of the upper half of the *ankh*. These small hardstone beads drilled with longitudinal and lateral holes are masterpieces of lapidary-work. It is probable that the so-called clasp is really a pendant or pectoral, judging from its shape, and the necklace was a continuous string of beads passed round the neck of the wearer and clasped on the breast by the pendant.

13   Bracelet, gold. D. 6·5 cm. IInd Dynasty. In the Metropolitan Museum of Art, New York, Reg. No. 01.4.2.

The bracelet, one of a pair, was excavated by Flinders Petrie in a chamber of the cenotaph or tomb of King Kha-sekhem-wy, the last king of the IInd Dynasty, at Abydos. The collapse of a wall had partially crushed it but also preserved it from the attention of thieves who ravaged the ancient burial grounds. It is of a design which is characteristic of the earliest dynasties (*cf.* Plate 3), probably being a metal version of an ivory archetype. The gold is thin, little better than foil, and may originally have been backed with plaster or clay which has entirely disappeared.

14   Bracelet, gold. L. c. 14 cm. IIIrd Dynasty. In the Cairo Museum.

In 1954, Zakaria Goneim, excavating the unfinished step-pyramid of King Sekhem-khet at Saqqara, found under fallen debris in a corridor beneath the superstructure what was evidently a robber's cache of gold objects stolen from the burial and never retrieved. The hoard included twenty-one graduated gold bracelets, similar to the type illustrated in Plate 13, a pair of tweezers in electrum and a handsome toilet box in the form of two gold scallop-shells connected by a hinge, the earliest example of such a device yet known. Goneim also recovered 388 hollow gold ball beads made by working sheet metal into a suitable hemispherical die and soldering the two resulting domes together. Also found with them were five gold perforated spacer-bars, two of which were broken and incomplete. Using these beads and spacers it was possible to reconstruct a bracelet or anklet of ten strings of traditional form (*cf.* Figs. 35, 36) with tie-cords acting as fasteners. The graduated bracelets found in this hoard are distinctly feminine, and the gold-work may therefore have been part of the funerary equipment of a woman of the royal house who was buried in the pyramid complex.

15 Relief, limestone, on the west wall of the offering-chamber of the mastaba of Khufu-Khaf (Nos. G. 7130 and 7140) at Giza. W. 76 cm., H. 61 cm. IVth Dynasty.
This portion of the scene shows the owner and his wife receiving the offerings brought to their tomb-chapel. She wears the classic Egyptian dress, a linen sheath supported by wide shoulder-straps. Her hair is shown cropped short since she has dispensed with her wig (*cf.* Plate 18). Her jewellery includes a choker of beads strung between spacers around her throat, and a set of graduated bracelets on each forearm (*cf.* Plates 3, 13).

16 Circlet, copper, gold leaf and coloured gesso. D. 18·5 cm., W. 3·1 cm., W. of roundels 11 cm. Excavated in tomb G 7143B at Giza. Vth Dynasty. In the Museum of Fine Arts, Boston (Mass.), Reg. No. 37.606A, B.
This circlet has been skilfully reconstructed from decayed fragments recovered by the Boston-Harvard Expedition from the burial of a woman. Like a specimen in Leipzig also from Giza, it shows a development of the jewel illustrated in Plate 4 in that the diadem has become a complete circlet. A characteristic of all such fillets is that the roundels stand some distance away from the band attached by rivets whose heads are concealed by carnelian bosses. The Boston circlet is a closed ring of sheet copper coated inside and out with gold leaf. Three ornaments are rivetted to this band, each based upon the 'bow-knot' design of two opposed papyrus umbels with a carnelian boss at their junction. Rising from the disk is an *ankh*-sign on either side of which a crested ibis roosts facing its companion: their beaks are crossed over the loop of the *ankh*. The central roundel carries an additional element pendant from its centre consisting of a five petalled flower flanked on each side by a bud, the whole probably representing the flowering rush seen on the circlet of Nofret (Plate 18) and the crown of Khnumet (Plate 27). The roundels are made by working thin copper sheet in repoussé so that the details stand out in relief on the face which is covered with a layer of linen in the hollows acting as a key for coloured gesso. The exposed parts of the metal were covered with gold leaf and in its original state the circlet must have given the impression of being fashioned of gold inlaid with coloured stones. It was therefore probably made exclusively for funerary use.

17 Relief, painted limestone, from the offering chamber of the mastaba of

Ptah-sekhem-ankh at Saqqara. Vth Dynasty. In the Museum of Fine Arts, Boston (Mass.), Reg. No. 04.1760.

The boatmen in their papyrus skiffs are sparring with each other using their poles as weapons, a not uncommon theme in reliefs of the Old Kingdom. The sport probably has some festal and religious significance for they have decked themselves liberally with lotus flowers, tucking some into the circlets around their heads and hanging others from long stalks like pectorals around their necks. Such ornaments were copied in less ephemeral and more precious substances (*cf.* Plate 34).

18 Upper part of the statue of the king's relation, Nofret, painted limestone from Meydum. Late IIIrd or early IVth Dynasty. In the Cairo Museum, Cat. No. 4.

Over her cropped poll (*cf.* Plate 15), Nofret wears a short bushy wig which is confined by a circlet painted in colours to suggest that the original was of silver inlaid with carnelian, lapis lazuli and turquoise (*cf.* Plate 39). The decoration is based upon the flowering rush and a rosette of eight petals (*cf.* Plate 27). Around her neck is a Broad Collar consisting of rows of carnelian, turquoise and lapis lazuli cylindrical beads and a lower border of drop-beads (*cf.* Plate 10).

19 Broad Collar, gold and faience. W. 34·5 cm. Excavated in the tomb of Impy at Giza. Later VIth Dynasty. In the Museum of Fine Arts, Boston (Mass). Reg. No. 13.3086.

This collar is a rare example found intact in the tomb of the owner. It is semi-circular in shape (*cf.* Plate 20) with but a modest graduation of the beads that form the body of the collar. These are of short, barrel shape in place of the more usual tubular type. The semi-circular end-pieces are inscribed with the name and titles of Impy and the drop-beads at the lower fringe take the form of stylized beetles (*cf.* Plate 4). This jewel was evidently made purely for funerary purposes. It consists of numerous ring and barrel beads in faience with gold adjuncts which have suffered little damage or shrinkage in the four thousand years of their existence and gives a good idea of what the imitations of expensive gold and cloisonné jewels looked like when they first left their makers' hands.

20–22 Jewellery of the Steward Wah, electrum, gold, silver, steatite and faience. XIth Dynasty. In the Metropolitan Museum of Art, New York.

The Egyptian Expedition of the Metropolitan Museum excavated the tomb of Wah at Deir el-Bahri in 1920, but his jewellery remained unsuspected until 1940 when they examined his wrapped mummy with X-rays (*cf.* Plate 117) and found that his personal ornaments were still in position on his body.

20 Broad Collar of the Steward Wah, faience. D. 39·4 cm. XIth Dynasty. M.M.A. Reg. No. 40.3.2.
The Broad Collar is made of bright blue-green faience beads and is in an excellent state of preservation being still on its original threads. It is of characteristic XIth Dynasty form being almost circular in shape and much deeper in the middle than at the ends.

21 Scarab necklace of the Steward Wah, gold, silver and steatite. L. (of scarab) 3·8 cm. XIth Dynasty. M.M.A. Reg. No. 40.3.12.
The amuletic beads are shown on their original string as they were found between the bandages of Wah. The scarab is among the earliest known and is remarkable for being made of solid silver built up from several parts soldered together with a gold tube running longitudinally through it to take the suspension cord. The back is inlaid in electrum with the names and titles of Wah and his patron, the Chancellor Meket-Re. The underside bears a design of scrolls and amuletic glyphs and gives evidence of having been worn in life. It was utilized as an amulet for the dead man by threading it on a string with a cylindrical and a barrel-shaped steatite bead for hanging around the neck (cf. Figs. 23, 24), though for this purpose its cord was too short and, like a smaller silver scarab and a third example in lapis lazuli, each accompanied by two beads, it was merely laid upon the breast of the deceased.

22 Necklaces of the Steward Wah, silver, gold, faience and hardstones. Average length 70 cm. XIth Dynasty. M.M.A. Reg. Nos. 40.3.15–19.
The five necklaces are exhibited on their original strings which were tied around the neck of Wah. From top to bottom they are of blue faience ball beads; tubular and barrel beads in carnelian, moss agate, milky quartz, black and white porphyry and green glazed steatite; hollow gold ball beads; blue faience ball beads; and large hollow silver ball beads. The metal beads have been made by beating heavy foil into hemispherical moulds, soldering tubes at each pole and joining the halves at their junctions. The thicker tie-cords of the first and last necklaces in the series should be noted.

23 Portion of a relief, limestone, with traces of paint. H. 31·8 cm., W. 29·9 cm. From the tomb of Queen Nofru at Deir el-Bahri, Thebes. XIth Dynasty. In a private collection.
The relief shows a procession of singing girls who are accompanying their chant with hand-claps. They wear the classic sheath dress, the white of its linen indicated by traces of pigment. The Broad Collars are delineated by spots of paint to represent the blue, green and red beads of the originals. The singers also wear long black wigs or coiffures with curious ornaments in the form of white disks threaded on strings. These probably represent silver hair ornaments of the same kind as those shown in Plate 6. Other

representations exist of hair and wig ornaments as at Meir and Qau (*cf.* Fig. 37), but none is so bold and detailed as this example.

24 Upper part of a statue of Queen Nofret, black granite. H. 70 cm. Found at Tanis in 1860–61. Middle XIIth Dynasty. In the Cairo Museum, Cat. No. 381.

Nofret, who was the chief queen of King Sesostris II, is shown in all her finery. She wears the heavy wig of the period confined by a snood of gold bands and wires. The ends of the two masses that fall on her breast are caught around bobbins which on the coffin of Seneb-tisi, are shown as carnelian bosses (*cf.* Plate 32). From her neck hangs on straps a pectoral with a design of her husband's cartouche flanked by crowned uraei in the upper half; and two *rekhyt*-birds, signifying the adoring populace of Egypt, confronting a *djed*-pillar beneath two *wedjet*-eyes in the lower half. On her wrists are bracelets with spacer-bars.

25–26 Pectoral, electrum, traces of inlay. H. 3·8 cm., L. 5·7 cm. XIIth Dynasty. Eton College, Windsor.

This pectoral, which is reputed to have come from Dahshur, has suffered some distortion and loss of inlays since it was first found and wrenched into two parts by those who wished to divide the spoil. Its two halves were previously in different collections but have recently been happily re-united under one ownership. The almost total loss of the inlays gives a good idea of how such jewels were made. The face exhibits the appearance of the metal frame before the pieces of stone, cut to shape and polished, were cemented in position. The reverse, here enlarged to twice its proper size, shows the delicate chasing of the details. The central element in the design is the head of the goddess Bat, with her cow ears and horns, from which hangs a garland ending in drop-beads (*cf.* Plates 2, 34). She supports a sun-disk with opposed uraei, probably signifying the Pharaoh, which are protected on either side by left and right *wedjet*-eyes of the sky-god Horus. From the lower bar, probably representing the earth, spring two papyrus plants to support the celestrial parts above (*cf.* Plate 41) and within the space so formed squat the two divine heraldic supporters of Upper and Lower Egypt, Horus as a hieracosphinx and Set as a lion with the head of the Set animal and an arrow-like tail. Two ribbed tubes act as anchorages for the suspensory cord.

27–31 Jewellery from the parure of the Princess Khnumet from Dahshur. (see also Plates 11, 12).

27 Circlet, gold inlaid with carnelian, lapis lazuli and turquoise. D. 20·5 cm., Max. H. 4·2 cm. In the Cairo Museum, Cat. No. 52860.

This crown is a translation into cloisonné-work of the type of fillet represented on the statue of Nofret (*cf.* Plate 18). The circlet is composed of eight identical elements, each consisting of a central rosette flanked by two stylized flowering rush calices and surmounted by such a device. Each of these components is separated from the next by another rosette. The inner surface of the gold band is chased with a design defining the various cloisons that on the front are filled with coloured stones. Between the centre of two of the elements is soldered an arch in the form of a flying vulture with its talons holding *shen*-signs (*cf.* Plates 102, 105). The wings and back of the bird are formed from a gold plate curved to shape, the details of the feathering being chased. The body, head and talons were made of separate parts soldered to this plate; the eyes are inlaid with obsidian. Opposite this vulture, which suggests that the owner had reached the status of a queen, is a socket to take a gold foil ornament, now much damaged, in the shape of a kind of palm tree. This finial took the place of the upright flickering plume which is sometimes found on the crowns of princesses, as for instance that of Sit-Hathor-Yunet (*cf.* Plates 39, 60).

28 Circlet, gold, carnelian, lapis lazuli and turquoise. D. 18 cm. In the Cairo Museum, Cat. No. 52859.
This is a gold cloisonné version of a circlet made by twisting a handful of water-weed into a chaplet (*cf. Fig.* 6). The wreath is caught at six points by a Maltese cross formed of four papyrus umbels around a central boss (*cf.* Plate 4). Each of these anchorages is connected to the next by ten wires which spring from three points in the thickness of the cross, three wires each from the upper and lower umbels, and four from the middle. These wires are interlaced in pairs through minute gold rings to which are soldered flowerettes, each with five turquoise-filled petals radiating from a carnelian centre, or pairs of lapis lazuli buds on gold wires. Each division carries about twenty-six flowers and nineteen pairs of buds. From the moment of its discovery, this chaplet has been admired as one of the triumphs of the Egyptian goldsmith, a happy combination of fragility and strength, of formalized flower shapes scattered in the random profusion of nature.

29 Pendant, necklaces, clasp and wig (?) ornaments, gold decorated with applied wires and grains. In the Cairo Museum, Cat. Nos. 52975–9.
Khnumet had among her possessions a suite of gold jewellery which has a distinctly un-Egyptian appearance in its designs and techniques. The art of attaching gold wires and granules to ornaments of gold by means of colloidal gold soldering appears to have been developed elsewhere, probably in Syria or the Aegean: further comment is offered below. As the 'Treasure of Tod' shows (see p. 33), trade relations with Asia during the XIIth Dynasty were close; and this group of goldwork may have been presented to Khnumet by an Asiatic ruler. Or, it may have been made by Egyptian jewellers under the direct inspiration of Asiatic or Aegean models. A third possibility is that it may have been made by immigrants from the Eastern

Mediterranean working in Egyptian studios. It is unique to Khnumet, with one minor exception (*cf.* Plate 46): her relatives had no jewels of this type among their parures.

Top: The pendant consists of a central element, the so-called 'Medallion of Dahshur' (D. 2·85 cm.), a circular plaque of blue frit on which is painted a recumbent cow (of Hathor?) with a garland hanging from its neck within a circle of black, brown and white segments. This miniature is covered by a thin plate of rock crystal retained by a circular gold frame decorated with granules. From the lower edge of the frame depend, by simple chains, three open-work, eight-pointed, stars decorated with granules. The medallion in turn hangs from two larger openwork rosettes, each with eight semi-circular projections also embellished with granules. The rayed medallion or star-shaped pendant is a distinctly Syrian motif.

Second Row: A necklace consisting of a length of double loop-in-loop chain, 28 cm. long, which has been broken and repaired in three places, and from which hang twelve gold pendants in the shape of stylized flies or bees. Similar ornaments have been found at Palaikastro, Crete, and on other Middle Minoan sites. The bee is a motif which is found both in the Aegean and in Egypt at this time. The fly appears a little later (see Plate 53).

Third Row: The clasp is in the form of a butterfly (W. 2·7 cm.) made from thin sheet gold on which the details of the insect's body and wing-membranes have been outlined in gold wire and soldered in position with granules filling the spaces so defined. To the back is soldered a channel to take the fastening bar sliding on a tongue within grooves. To each part is connected a length of double loop-in-loop chain. While the butterfly is a Minoan motif, it had also existed in Egypt as a design of a jewel at least as early as the IVth Dynasty (*cf.* Plate 3). The shape of this butterfly resembles Egyptian examples rather than Aegean congeners.

Bottom Row: The necklace consists of a portion of double loop-in-loop chain from which is suspended ten bivalve cockle-shells and two star-shaped pendants (W. of latter, 2·5 cm.) by means of short links. The shells have been made by burnishing gold foil into an appropriate open, hemispherical mould, chasing in the striations and soldering the two halves together probably with a fine clay filling retained within (*cf.* Plate 78). The stars have been made by outlining the central circle and profile in gold wire and filling the areas so defined with granules. The five-pointed star is an Egyptian celestial motif, but here it may represent a starfish. Shell pendants are characteristic of the Nubian area, being traded from the Red Sea; but they became popular in Egypt during the Middle Kingdom (see Plate 45).

All the jewels in this group as catalogued and exhibited are incomplete and in view of their unique nature it is unlikely that companion pieces were stolen by de Morgan's workmen to find their way into the antiquities market, though odd lengths of gold chain may have disappeared. It seems logical to postulate, therefore, that either a total of two complete necklaces in granular gold-work were all that was included in Khnumet's deposit, and the two upper and the two lower examples on this plate belong together; or else, that portions of four necklaces, broken in use and kept in her trinket boxes, were buried with her.

Sides: Ornaments in the form of small birds, each 1·1 cm. high, made by working gold foil into an appropriate mould and soldering a flat plate to the back, the edges being trimmed. Two holes in the lower part allowed for the passage of air during heating and cooling and were the means of attaching them, doubtless to a wig (*cf.* Plate 6).

30 Collar, gold, inlaid with carnelian, lapis lazuli and turquoise. H. (of terminals) 1·3 cm., W. 1·1 cm. In the Cairo Museum, Cat. Nos. 52920–21 *et al.*

This Falcon Collar has been reconstructed from elements nearly all of which have a right and left aspect, thus indicating that they formed pairs in some balanced arrangement. They also have a generic resemblance being of the same heights and made of gold, chased on their backs, and inlaid with coloured stones on their faces. The central element (H. 1·6 cm.) is an *ankh* upon an offering-mat and this is flanked in turn by hieroglyphs symbolizing deities, such as 'The Two Ladies' (*i.e.* the vulture of Upper Egypt and the cobra of Lower Egypt on *neb*-baskets), the goddess Bat, the King of Lower Egypt, and such abstractions as 'Life', 'Union', 'Strength', 'Stability', 'Protection'. The drop beads are inlaid in the same three coloured stones. The falcon-head terminals have rings at their vertices for taking the tie-cords. While the reconstruction of this collar from elements previously catalogued separately is entirely plausible, the order of stringing is largely arbitrary.

31 *Upper Row:* Four 'motto-clasps', gold inlaid with carnelian, turquoise and lapis lazuli. H. (left to right) 1·7 cm., 1·9 cm., 3·3 cm., 2·0 cm. In the Cairo Museum, Cat. Nos. 52914, 52955–6, 52958.

It seems to have been the fashion for the princesses of the XIIth Dynasty to wear an amuletic cloisonné jewel attached to a cord on the upper arm. Here the cords have been restored by strings of gold beads (*cf.* Plate 44). Each jewel is composed of a single sign or group of hieroglyphs spelling out a good wish. The cords were knotted into tubes on the back of each jewel, one being fixed, the other detachable and sliding on a tongue within grooves. The first two clasps read, 'all protection and life is at her back'. The next perhaps signifies a protective *meset*-apron; the last reads, 'joy'.

Lower Row: Girdle (?), gold, carnelian, lapis lazuli and turquoise. L. (doubled) 30 cm. In the Cairo Museum, no Cat. No.

Part of what was probably a girdle of 'acacia seed' beads placed around the body of Khnumet.

32 Painted limestone relief of Sit-hedj-hotpe and Sit-kheper-ka, two of the
daughters of Djehuti-hotpe, the powerful feudal lord of the 'Hare' district
of Middle Egypt who died in the reign of Sesostris III, *c.* 1850 BC. In the
Cairo Museum. H. 27·5 cm.
This fragment of wall from the tomb chapel of Djehuti-hotpe at Deir el-
Bersha gives a good idea of the full parure of women of high rank in the
middle years of the XIIth Dynasty. Each daughter wears her hair plumped
out in a bouffant mass on either side of the face. Such coiffures are kept in
place by gold bands, a lower carnelian terminal and a circlet probably of
beadwork, but possibly of cloisonné-work (*cf.* Plate 24). The bow-knot is a
plain disk, flanked by lotus flowers, and having two streamers hanging
from it of unequal length (*cf.* Plate 83). From the neck hangs a pectoral on
beadwork straps to fall low on the breast. It is of trapezoidal shape and is
evidently of gold inlaid with a device based upon the sun-disk encircled by
two opposed uraei wearing the Red Crown of Lower Egypt. The girls'
arms and legs are decorated with bracelets and anklets also in beadwork.
The white spacers on all these ornaments may be intended to represent
silver or electrum.

33, 34 Jewellery of the Princess Sit-Hathor, excavated by J. de Morgan near the
brick pyramid of Sesostris III at Dahshur.

33 *Centre:* Pectoral and necklace, gold inlaid with carnelian, lapis lazuli and
turquoise. H. (of pectoral) 5·2 cm. In the Cairo Museum, Cat. No. 52001
et al.
The Princess Sit-Hathor was a daughter of Sesostris II who gave her some of
her jewellery early in her adult life: other ornaments were bestowed upon
her by her brother or husband, Sesostris III, near whose brick pyramid at
Dahshur she was buried. This pectoral belongs to her earlier years and its
design is based upon the titles and names of Sesostris II contained within the
primeval shrine or kiosk in which the Creator (the ancestor of the Pharaoh)
manifested himself. The method of making all these pectorals is the same.
The design was drawn on a flat gold plate and was worked in low relief by
the chasing and repoussé techniques, (see p. 71). Thin strips of metal outlining the design were then soldered to the back of the plate which thereafter became the front of the jewel. Surplus metal was punched out, the
edges and contours trimmed and smoothed, and separate elements, such as
legs and suspension rings, soldered in position. Finally the cells were filled
with pieces of coloured stone cut and polished before they were cemented.
The design shows the sky-god Horus, of whom the king is an incarnation,
as a falcon wearing the Upper and Lower Egyptian crowns, standing upon a
collar symbolizing his victory over Set, the god of violence, and supporting the prenomen of Sesostris II surmounted by his 'Golden Horus' name.

The sun-disk, encircled by a uraeus which embraces an *ankh*-sign of life further supplements Horus, fills an empty space and strengthens the design. The workmanship of this jewel is impeccable (*cf.* Plate 37). The necklace on which it is suspended has been restored with assurance as a result of Winlock's researches. Its beads have been selected from a mass haphazardly recovered by de Morgan.

Outer: Girdle of Sit-Hathor, gold, lapis lazuli, green felspar. L. *c.* 70 cm. In the Cairo Museum. Cat. No. 53136, 53123 *et al.*

The girdle has been restored as a result of the study of the El-Lahun specimen (*cf.* Plate 35). Some of its parts, however, were stolen at the time of discovery by de Morgan's workmen, and it is thus shorter than it should be. This cowrie-shell girdle is a good example of a type of jewel that belongs to the middle years of the XIIth Dynasty which was then superseded by another design (see Plate 36).

34 Jewellery of Sit-Hathor, gold, carnelian, lapis lazuli, green felspar, turquoise. In the Cairo Museum, Cat. Nos. 53137, 52041–2, 53141, 53150, 53142.

Top: Bracelet, L. 20 cm. Three of the XIIth Dynasty princesses had bracelets containing a pair of couchant lions, some threaded on double strings, and some on single strings of beads (*cf.* Plate 44). One of Sit-Hathor's examples shown here is reconstructed after the Lahun specimens. The couchant lions were made in halves by burnishing gold foil onto a core and soldering the two shells longitudinally along their seams. The complete animal was soldered to a thick base-plate which is perforated to allow the double threads to run through. The beads are of gold, carnelian and turquoise strung with a gold knot terminal in two halves forming a clasp.

Left and Right: Bracelet clasps, gold inlaid with carnelian, lapis lazuli and turquoise. H. 3·9 cm. These fasteners from a pair of Sit-Hathor's wide bracelets should be compared with those in Plates 12 and 46.

Each slide is decorated with a *djed*-pillar worked *à jour*, chased on its back and inlaid on its face. Two of the end-spacers of the bracelets are shown in position on the tongues of the slides: each was perforated with thirty-six holes corresponding to the number of strings of beads in the bracelets.

Centre, top and bottom: Clasp, gold inlaid with carnelian, other inlays now missing. L. 3·7 cm. The centre of the clasp is formed by a knot in gold consisting of two halves which slide together on a tongue and groove (*cf.* Plate 36). From the knot falls on either side the stalk of a papyrus umbel, each furnished with three rings to take the threads of a three-string necklace.

'Motto clasp', gold inlaid with carnelian and lapis lazuli. H. 1·8 cm. A clasp similar to those shown in Plate 31 consisting of a rebus of hieroglyphs reading, 'the two gods [Horus and Set] are at peace'. Clasps designed to express the same idea are found in other royal deposits of the period, and nearly all have lost the greater part of their inlays (*cf.* Plate 44)·

Clasp, gold inlaid with carnelian, lapis lazuli and turquoise. H. 2·7 cm.
Two lotus flowers in cloisonné-work with their stalks tied in a knot above the 'aegis' of the goddess Bat form the main design. The head of Bat, shown full face with cow ears, is surmounted by two loops instead of horns (*cf.* Plate 26). From her neck hangs a pectoral ending in drop-beads. Tubular anchorages for cords are on the reverse, one of them, sliding on a tongue, is detachable. Small rings are soldered on the back of the flowers presumably to take bead pendants representing buds. The clasp has been restrung on a bracelet of gold ring beads.

35–40 Jewellery of the Princess Sit-Hathor-Yunet excavated by G. Brunton and Flinders Petrie in a tomb within the precincts of the pyramid complex of Sesostris II at Lahun, and now mostly in New York. The contents of the jewellery caskets were recovered completely; and brilliantly reconstructed by H. E. Winlock of the Metropolitan Museum of Art, New York, using the notes and diagrams made by Brunton during his painstaking recovery of this treasure found buried in about a cubic yard of stirred-up mud (see pp. 10–11).

35 Girdle of Sit-Hathor-Yunet, gold, carnelian, lapis lazuli, green felspar. L. 84 cm. In New York, M.M.A. Reg. No. 16.1.5.
The girdle consists of eight hollow gold beads in the form of cowries, one of which is made in two parts and fastens together by a tongue engaging in a slot to form the clasp. These are threaded on two strings alternating with groups of twelve 'acacia-seed' beads in carnelian, lapis lazuli, green felspar and gold, the last being soldered in pairs to form spacers. The shells are of gold hammered over a wood or stone positive and finished by chasing. Two halves made in this way were soldered along their seams. Each cowrie is double sided showing lips on both faces. A few rattling pellets of a copper-silver alloy are contained in each shell so that the wearer must have tinkled as she walked like the 'daughters of Zion'. Other women of the royal house had similar girdles (*cf.* Plates 33, 45) which have survived only in part. Their design appears to be characteristic of the earlier half of the XIIth Dynasty, and this particular example was therefore probably made in the reign of Sesostris II.

36 Girdle and claw anklets of Sit-Hathor-Yunet, gold and amethyst. L. (girdle) 82 cm., L. (anklets) 17·5 cm. In New York, M.M.A. Reg. Nos. 16.1.6, 7.
In addition to her cowrie-shell girdle, Sit-Hathor-Yunet had a second girdle, probably made for her in a later reign, in which the eight gold cowrie shells were replaced by seven double-sided, hollow gold beads in the form of opposed leopard heads—a device which appears to have had a

protective significance. These were threaded on a double string of dark amethyst ball beads caught at intermediate points by gold spacer-beads made in the form of miniature versions of the large leopard-head beads and soldered in pairs. The construction of the hollow gold beads is precisely similar to that of the cowrie-shell beads in the earlier girdle, one bead being made in two halves sliding together on a tongue in a groove to form a fastener. A number of stone pellets were included in each bead to act as rattles.

The claw anklets were evidently made *en suite*, using the same dark purple colour of amethyst for the ball beads. Each claw is of gold, much simpler in design than Khnumet's inlaid pair (*cf.* Plate 12), but is surmounted by two hollow gold ball beads soldered together and to the middle of the cap, showing that the anklets consisted of a double row of beads. Each has been supplied with a single gold knot fastener. Queen Mereret who was buried at Dahshur (*cf.* Plate 44) also had a similar gold and amethyst girdle with eight large leopard-head rattles, but with no small example of such beads: it remains to be reconstructed.

37 Pectoral of Sit-Hathor-Yunet, gold inlaid with carnelian, lapis lazuli and turquoise. H. 4·5 cm. In New York, M.M.A. Reg. No. 16.1.3.

This jewel, together with the contemporary pectoral of Sit-Hathor (see Plate 33), probably represents the acme of the jeweller's art in Ancient Egypt. Its construction is similar to that of Sit-Hathor's example except that the primeval kiosk is replaced by a base-bar with a zig-zag inlay representing the Waters of Chaos from which Creation arose. Two falcons, each wearing on its vertex the sun-disk encircled by a uraeus with a pendant *ankh*, protect the prenomen of King Sesostris II, which is supported by a kneeling personification of Eternity holding notched palm-ribs to signify a count of years. The whole design symbolizes that the divine power that created the universe is incarnate in the Pharaoh.

The mirror placed at the back of the pectoral in this illustration gives some idea of the quality of the chasing on the gold back-plate where the feathering of the birds has been indicated by lines of almost microscopic fineness (see Plate 73). This pendant was hung around the neck on a necklace of drop and ball beads similar to those shown in Plates 33, 41, and 42.

38 Pectoral, gold inlaid with carnelian, lapis lazuli, green faience and amethyst. W. 8·2 cm. In the Cairo Museum, Cat. No. 52712.

Sit-Hathor-Yunet's second pectoral is a copy of the earlier one and was made for her in the reign of Ammenemes III whose name replaces that of Sesostris II in the cartouche upheld by Eternity. During the forty years or more that separate the date of the two jewels, however, there are signs of a decline in the standards and skill of the Court jewellers, unless this is the work of an inferior craftsman who was given an earlier pattern to follow (but *cf.* Plate 42). The falcons are clumsy and earth-bound when compared with those of Sesostris II and the chasing of the back-plate is coarser and less detailed (see Plate 74). The colour scheme is also different, the sun-disks being of red carnelian, and the eyes of amethyst instead of garnet. Ball beads of amethyst instead of lapis lazuli were also used for the suspensory necklace. An artificial substance, probably green faience or frit, has been used in place of turquoise or green felspar, and this, in the damp mud in which it was buried for so long, has decayed to a white powdery substance.

39 Wig ornaments, gold, and gold inlaid with carnelian, lapis lazuli and green faience. Originals in the Cairo Museum, Cat. No. 52641, and New York, M.M.A. Reg. No. 31.10.8.
    The ornaments, here seen mounted on a modern version of a wig of the period, are a reproduction of the 'boatman's circlet' (see p. 130) worn by Sit-Hathor-Yunet, now in Cairo, and the original gold tubes that were threaded on her tresses in a chequer-pattern (*cf.* Plate 6). Fifteen rosettes made in cloisonné-work are rivetted at intervals to the band of the circlet which is 2·7 cm. wide. Each rosette consists essentially of a quatrefoil based on the design of a flowering rush, but in the original only the red carnelian inlays remain, the blue and green faience or frit inlays have decayed to a white powder. Three of the rosettes, one on each side and one at the back, are furnished with rings to which are hinged streamers of plain gold sheet. On the upper edge at the back in place of the usual knot (*cf.* Plate 32) is a papyrus umbel worked in the round from which springs a flickering plume of gold sheet similiar in design to the streamers but inverted. The place of a rosette at the front of the crown is taken by a detachable uraeus worked *à jour* with a head of lapis lazuli and eyes of garnet set in gold rims.

40 Bracelet of Sit-Hathor-Yunet, gold, carnelian and turquoise. H. 8·1 cm. In New York, M.M.A. Reg. No. 16.1.8.
    The bracelet unclasped and laid flat gives a good idea of the construction and appearance of such jewels during the Middle Kingdom (*cf.* Plate 49). Each bracelet, worn at the wrist, consists of a band of thirty-seven rows of carnelian and turquoise beads strung on threads between two gold end-pieces each of box-construction, one face being cut with a slot. The strings are held together at intervals by six gold spacer-bars comprising tubular beads soldered to a back-plate. The slide, which forms a red element in the alternation of red and green vertical stripes, is provided with a T-shaped tongue along each long side. It connects the two end-pieces of the bracelet by engaging in their slots. The face of each slide is inscribed with a title and name of Ammenemes III in cloisonné-work, originally inlaid with blue and green faience or frit which has decomposed to a white substance (*cf.* Pl. 75).

41, 42, Jewellery of Queen Mereret, excavated by J. de Morgan, near the brick
44–46, pyramid of Sesostris III at Dahshur. XIIth Dynasty.

41 Pectoral of Queen Mereret, gold inlaid with carnelian, lapis lazuli and turquoise. W. 8·5 cm. In the Cairo Museum, Cat. No. 52002 *et al.*
Within the primeval shrine, which has its cornice supported by a lotus flower on a slender stalk, King Sesostris III, in the form of a pair of opposed hieracosphinxes wearing the *Ibes* crown, tramples a Libyan and a Nubian underfoot—a theme common in Egyptian iconography showing the Pharaoh dominant over the contiguous nations. The outstretched paws of the sphinxes are on the heads of the subjugated and support the prenomens of the king. The vulture goddess Nekhebet of Upper Egypt, holding *shen*-signs in her claws, spreads protective wings over the entire scene. The workmanship of this piece is still excellent but the design is rather less effective than that of the earlier examples. The lotus flower turned inwards to strengthen the jewel mechanically, is not too happily placed. The necklace has been restored from a mass of beads gathered at the time of discovery.

42 Pectoral of Queen Mereret, gold inlaid with carnelian, lapis lazuli and faience or frit. W. 10·4 cm. In the Cairo Museum, Cat. No. 52003 *et al.*
This is a jewel of similar type to that shown in Plate 41 but made for the queen by the successor of Sesostris III. The primeval kiosk is of simple design, with its base and support decorated with a block-border and upholding a cavetto cornice. Over the scene hovers the vulture Nekhebet with protective wings outspread holding the signs of life and stability in her talons. Below, in opposed halves, King Ammenemes III, wearing a *khat* wig-cover and an archaic kilt and tunic, raises his mace to strike down bedouin foes shown kneeling helpless before him, each holding a throw-stick and a dagger. The prenomen of the king in a cartouche is before him, and at his back is a fan-bearer in the form of an animated *ankh*-sign. The various elements in the design are held together with descriptive hieroglyphic labels. Nekhebet is entitled 'Mistress of The Two Lands, Lady of Heaven'; the king is 'The Good God, Lord of the Two Lands'; and the action he is performing is 'subjugating all foreign lands', and 'smiting the bedouin of Asia'. Such fussy connecting links disturb the design and give the jewel a confused surface appearance (see also Plate 76). The workmanship is inferior to earlier pectorals of the XIIth Dynasty and the artificial substitute for turquoise or green felspar has decayed to a brownish or white substance. The necklace has been strung from beads gathered from the same deposit (*cf.* Plate 41).

43 Uraeus of Sesostris II, gold, inlaid with carnelian, lapis lazuli and green felspar. H. 5·5 cm. In the Cairo Museum, Cat. No. 52702.
This jewel was found by G. Brunton as a result of sifting the dust and rubble

that covered the floor of a chamber in the king's pyramid at Lahun. There is little doubt that this emblem of the king's personal deity that was supposed to spit fire in the eyes of his enemy, was actually attached to one of the crowns of Sesostris II. The body is of gold made by hammering heavy sheet and soldering on the details. The head is carved from a piece of lapis lazuli with eyes of garnet set in gold rims. The body, of hollow section, makes an S-turn before tapering to an undulating tail. Two rings are soldered along the middle line to the back of the hollow body for sewing the uraeus to a cloth or leather head-dress.

44–46   Jewellery from the burial of Queen Mereret. In the Cairo Museum.

44   *Top:* Pendant, gold inlaid with carnelian and blue and green faience. W. 3·3 cm. Cat. No. 53078.
The pendant is in the form of a falcon with outspread wings holding *shen*-signs in its talons. Of the inlays, only the carnelian has retained its colour, the rest have decayed to a white paste; some are missing. Two rings are soldered to the backplate to take a necklace: below the tail are two rings to take a further pendant which has not been identified among the jewels haphazardly recovered from Mereret's deposit.
Sides: Bracelets, gold, carnelian and turquoise. L. *c.* 16·5 cm. Cat. No. 53096–9.
A pair of lion bracelets similar to that belonging to Sit-Hathor in Plate 34, except that the lions are perforated with a single hole emerging from between the two forepaws and under the tail. They were therefore threaded on a single string of beads fitted with a gold knot clasp.
Centre (inner): Five 'motto' clasps, gold inlaid with carnelian and discoloured pastes. W. 1 to 3·3 cm. Cat. Nos. 53076, 53079–82.
These clasps are of the same type and construction as those belonging to Khnumet in Plate 31, and Sit-Hathor in Plate 34. The blue and green inlays, as was so often the case with the jewellery of the later years of the XIIth Dynasty, were of faience or frit which has decayed to a greenish, brown or white paste. All are furnished with the usual fasteners to take cords at the rear; and, in addition, three have ring beads at intervals along the lower bar for the suspension of further elements. The 'mottos' are, (top) the *shen*-sign signifying the entire circuit of the sun over which the Pharaoh ruled; 'joy' and 'the two gods are at peace': this last is arranged upside down on the plate.
Centre (outer): A necklace, gold, carnelian, lapis lazuli and turquoise. L. *c.* 35 cm. Cat. Nos. 53069, 53083.
A necklace reconstructed from random elements found in the tomb of Queen Mereret. The pendants are formed of eight turquoise, five carnelian and five lapis lazuli balls, each held in a cage formed of two large circles of

gold strip over the gathered ends of which is forced a striated tube of gold foil soldered at the upper extremity. One end is prolonged into a loop and soldered to form a ring by which the pendant is hung on a string of similar gold beads. The clasp is in the form of a motto with two *sa*-signs flanking an *ankh* standing on a basket, the whole reading 'all protection and life' (*cf.* Plate 31). The usual slides at the back of the clasp take small tubes into which the ends of the necklace are knotted.

45   *Outer*: Girdle of Queen Mereret, gold. L. (of each shell) 5·7 cm. Cat. Nos. 53074, 53165.
The eight cowrie shells were made in the same manner as those of similar girdles belonging to the women of the royal house at this period (*cf.* Plate 35). One of the shells is made in two halves that slide together to form a clasp. Queen Mereret had two or more imitation cowrie shell girdles in her parure, but as parts were pilfered at the time of discovery, it is impossible to say how they should be reconstructed. It may well be that the smaller gold cowries belong to an entirely separate girdle composed of beads strung on two threads.
Inner, top: Pendant, gold inlaid with carnelian, lapis lazuli and turquoise. H. 4·6 cm. Cat. No. 53070.
The pendant is made in imitation of a trimmed pearl shell and is inlaid at its top with a design based on the lotus flower from which hangs a wreath of stylized flower petals, ending in a pendant of three chevrons, all in cloisonné-work.
Inner, middle: Part of a collar, gold. L. *c.* 10 cm. Cat. No. 53171.
The collar consists of a number of rectangular gold elements, each built up from groups of three ring beads soldered at intervals to a vertical bar and spaced in threes along tubes of smaller diameter. To the lower edge of the middle of some of these elements is soldered a bivalve shell, 0·8 cm. high. The gold spacers were probably strung on a necklace of three strings alternating with coloured stone beads similar to a collar found on the body of Seneb-tisi. Khnumet also had a similar, but simpler, ornament of small bivalve shells, strung on a necklace of beads.
Inner, bottom: Gold shell. W. 7·6 cm. Cat. No. 53255.
A pendant in the form of a bivalve shell beaten out of a disk of massive gold with a suspension ring soldered to the hollow back, at the apex. The originals of such ornaments made of pearl shells trimmed to shape and often inscribed with the king's name were commonly worn in Egypt during the Middle Kingdom and seem to be of Nubian inspiration.

46   *Outer* (above): Two cylindrical pendants, gold, lapis lazuli and turquoise. L. 4·9 cm. and 5·3 cm. Cat. Nos. 53071–2.
These curious pendants consist essentially of gold cylindrical boxes fitted with caps furnished with suspension rings. The one on the right is skilfully

decorated with chevrons in granular work (*cf.* Plate 29); the example on the left has inlays set between cloisons formed by gold rings. The purpose of such objects is unknown; but they are generally thought to have contained an amulet of some sort, evidently of perishable material.

Outer (below): A pair of bracelet slides, gold inlaid with carnelian, and turquoise. H. 6·4 cm. Cat. Nos. 52026–7.

Queen Mereret received from Ammenemes III two bracelets, similar to those of Sit-Hathor-Yunet, with slides inlaid with his name. For further details see Plates 40, 75.

Centre (above): Three finger rings, gold, carnelian, turquoise, amethyst. L. 1·1, 1·0, 1·8 cm. Cat. Nos. 52260, 52240, 52244.

The bezel of each ring is in the form of a scarab, one in amethyst, another in cloisonné-work on a plain gold base-plate, and a third in lapis lazuli mounted on a gold base-plate inscribed with the name and titles of Ammenemes III. Each scarab swivels on a gold wire ring, the ends of which are coiled about each other, a metal version of a simple linen thread tie.

Centre (below): Two hollow gold beads of the goddess Bat, from the inlays on the lid of one of Mereret's decayed jewellery caskets. (*cf.* Plate 152). W. 2·5 cm. Cat. Nos. 53094–5.

47 Strings of beads from private burials of the Middle Kingdom. In the Royal Scottish Museum, Edinburgh, Reg. Nos. 1907.713.7; 1914.1088–91, 1095. *From the top downwards:*

(a) A necklace of blue faience ball beads with natural shell terminals, from Rifa. L. 40·6 cm.

(b) A necklace of carnelian, amethyst, lapis lazuli and green felspar ball beads, from Haraga. L. 91·5 cm.

(c) A necklace of ribbed barrel beads and plain drop beads in carnelian, from Haraga. L. 24 cm.

(d) A bracelet of ribbed barrel beads in plaster-filled gold foil, from Haraga. L. 17·7 cm.

(e) A necklace of ribbed barrel beads in carnelian, lapis lazuli and turquoise, from Haraga. L. 34·5 cm.

(f) A necklace of thin barrel beads in carnelian, lapis lazuli and turquoise, from Haraga. L. 137 cm.

The hardstone beads buried with private persons during the Middle Kingdom and usually worn by them in life are often of high quality, as the selection in this plate will show.

48 Parure of an unknown woman, gold and electrum. Late XVIIth Dynasty. In the Royal Scottish Museum, Edinburgh. Reg. Nos. 1909.527.15–19.

In 1909 Flinders Petrie excavating at Qurna, near the mouth of the Valley of the Kings at Western Thebes, found the intact burial of a woman and infant in a shallow grave cut in the rock. In this area several burials of the late

XVIIth and early XVIIIth Dynasties have been uncovered including those of the ruling family at Thebes. The richness of the parure discovered by Petrie is unusual for such an impoverished age and suggests that the woman and her child were important members of the royal house at Thebes towards the end of the XVIIth Dynasty, but her crude feathered coffin, despite its gold-leaf embellishment, was not inscribed with the name and titles of the deceased.

Top row: A pair of ear-rings, each 2–3 cm. in diameter, consisting of four penannular hoops soldered together, the two inner hoops having a smaller gap and so forming a tongue for penetrating the hole in the ear-lobe. Each hoop is made by soldering a number of rings together around a cylindrical former. Each ring is bent into a circle from a wire of triangular section made by cutting a thick gold sheet into strips with a chisel having a wide-angled bevel (see Fig. 18). The finished hoops have the appearance of being ribbed. These are the earliest examples of ear-rings in Ancient Egypt, the wearing of such ornaments evidently being an Asiatic fashion imported into Egypt in Hyksos times. An Asiatic oil-horn was also deposited among the grave-goods of this woman, perhaps suggesting that she may have been of foreign origin. According to Petrie the weights of her goldwork conform closely to a Syrian unit.

Centre, at sides: Four plain gold bangles worn as bracelets on both forearms; each 6 cm. in diameter and made up of gold bar of D-section bent into a circle and soldered.

Centre: A *shebyu*-collar with an outer circumference of 38 cm., consisting of four rows of gold rings threaded on a thick pad of fibre, the centre strings of which are knotted into the terminals. Each of these consists of eight rings soldered together to form a tube and four such tubes are soldered side by side. A perforated hemispherical cup carrying a ring is soldered at one end of each tube. When the two terminals are brought in juxtaposition the rings in the hemispheres are in alignment and allow a locking pin to be inserted between them. Each ring was made from wire of triangular section by a process similar to that used for the ear-rings. This jewel appears to be an early form of the *shebyu*-collar so often given as an award of honour by the Pharaohs to their subjects in the ensuing dynasty (see Plates 117, 118, 120).

Bottom row: A girdle of electrum beads, L. 79 cm., consisting of twenty-six cowroid shapes alternating with twelve barrel beads threaded on a double string. The larger beads have been described as copied from a disk of leather folded over and stitched; presumably such phylacteries contained charms written on pieces of papyrus, but no actual example has yet come to light.

49–58 Jewels from the parure of Queen Ah-hotpe deposited with her mummy in a huge coffin excavated in 1859 by Mariette's agents in the plain below the Dira Abu l'Naga, near the mouth of the Valley of the Kings at Western

Thebes (see pp. 9, 10). Ah-hotpe was the mother of Ka-mose and Amosis, the Theban princes who in succession fought a war of liberation against their Hyksos overlords ruling in Lower Egypt. The eventual triumph of Amosis ushered in a new period of prosperity and high culture for the Egyptians—the XVIIIth Dynasty which, with the two following dynasties, forms the era of the New Kingdom in Ancient Egypt. Queen Ah-hotpe was praised during her life-time for seizing the initiative and rallying the Theban forces at a critical juncture in their struggle against the Hyksos, probably on the death of her husband or her son, Ka-mose. Her honours in such a war-like age naturally included parade weapons and military decorations. Her burial regalia comprised jewels given to her by Ka-mose and by Amosis, late in whose reign she evidently died. The workmanship of these jewels is generally much cruder than that of the Middle Kingdom craftsmen but details of style and an improvement in the quality of some of the jewels given to Ah-hotpe by Amosis suggests that he fell heir to the experience and traditions of the Memphite studios. Among these craftsmen in the northern capital there must have been men who were influenced by the work of gold-smiths in other areas of the Eastern Mediterranean, for a dagger and parade-axe of Amosis have distinctly Helladic features in their decoration. Such foreign influences were to leave their impress on some of the design and details of jewellery during the New Kingdom.

49 *Left and centre:* A pair of bracelets or anklets, gold, carnelian, lapis lazuli and turquoise. L. (unclasped) 15·0 cm. H. 4·3 cm. In the Cairo Museum, Cat. Nos. 52071–2.

This jewel is constructed on entirely different principles from its Middle Kingdom counterparts. Firstly, the beads are strung on thirty gold wires, not threads, and have therefore retained their original order. The band, however, is only partly flexible. Secondly, the end-pieces, made in the form of lidless boxes, are fitted with perforated lugs that engage with each other and are locked by a retractable pin passing through their holes when in alignment. Thirdly, the spacers are formed of five gold elements each consisting of a strip with its long edges turned up and perforated to ride on the wires. The cylindrical beads are threaded in square groups each bisected diagonally to form triangles, one of which is of gold. Some of these groups fall within the confines of the gold spacers. The diagonal motif is very common at this period and appears on other jewels of Queen Ah-hotpe (*cf.* Plate 51). The end-pieces, when joined with their pins, show the names and titles of Amosis, 'beloved of Amun' and 'of Re,' chased on the outer surface, his prenomen on one complete clasp, his nomen on the other. In the plate, this pair of bracelets has been arranged upside down.

Right: Bracelet, gold, carnelian, lapis lazuli and turquoise. L. (laid flat) 16·5 cm. In the Cairo Museum. Cat. No. 52070.

This bracelet, or anklet, one of a pair, follows a more traditional method of manufacture except that eighteen wires are used as threads and the clasp fastens by means of a retractable pin engaging in catches on the end-pieces. The seven gold spacer-bars resemble Middle Kingdom prototypes (*cf.* Plate 40) but are not backed by a flat plate, and have four instead of three ring beads to each tubular unit. An eighth spacer-bar takes a different form, being of box form and having hieroglyphs in silhouette soldered to its outer face with the background filled in with pieces of lapis lazuli cut roughly to shape and cemented in position with mastic. These eight spacers alternate with nine vertical bars of beads in three colours. The fastening is similar in design to the examples on the specimens illustrated on the left, but the bracelet has been enlarged by interposing a plain gold bar carrying appropriate lugs on its long edges and locking in position with two retractable pins.

50   Pectoral, gold, inlaid with carnelian, lapis lazuli and turquoise. W. 9·2 cm. In the Cairo Museum, Cat. No. 52004.

This pectoral is made by the same technique as the Middle Kingdom examples (*cf.* Plate 33), but is far less accomplished, though the chasing of the reverse is a little more skilful than the lapidary work on the face. The kiosk has a base decorated with vertical zig-zags symbolizing the Waters of Heaven on which a solar bark floats protected by falcons flying above left and right. Within this craft a ceremony is taking place to which the name of 'The Baptism of Pharaoh' has been applied. In the centre, King Amosis is being lustrated by the falcon-headed Re of Lower Egypt and Amun of Upper Egypt who pour streams of water over him from the libation vases raised on high in their hands. The design is tied together by inscriptions (*cf.* Plate 42) which give the names and titles of Amosis and describe him as 'beloved of Re' and 'beloved of Amun-Re'. This jewel was probably made for the coronation of Amosis, one of the ceremonies of which was the purification of the king by priests impersonating the deities of the Four Quarters. Here, as usual, the rite is regarded as taking place in Heaven.

51, 52   Armlet, gold inlaid with carnelian, lapis lazuli and green felspar. W. 11 cm., H. 8·1 cm. In the Cairo Museum, Cat. No. 52642.

From the moment that this jewel was found, according to the report, in Queen Ah-hotpe's hair, it has been described as a crown. But it is undoubtedly a bracelet, its diameter showing that it could be slipped over the wrist and elbow and worn on the upper arm. The design is a development of the lion bracelets of the Middle Kingdom (*cf.* Plates 34 and 44). King Ka-mose had an armlet consisting of a box-like cartouche bearing his name and two lions (now in the Louvre) that evidently had been strung on a thick double cord encircling his upper arm. Here the combination has been translated into an inflexible gold armlet, half the gold circlet being worked by the repoussé technique into the semblance of a double twisted cord. The other half is planished flat and decorated by alternate *djed* and *tyet* symbols in cloisonné-work. From the centre of the circlet, opposite the cartouche, a tongue projects decorated in inlays with a feather-pattern. In use, it lay along the inner side of the arm to prevent the heavy cartouche and sphinxes from twisting the armlet round on the wearer. The sphinxes are made by hammering gold foil into a mould, or over a positive, and soldering the two shells along their longitudinal seam. Their head-dresses are formed of several plates soldered on separately and decorated in cloisonné-work, though many of the inlays have fallen out. The cartouche is made in the form of a box, the sides being decorated with a characteristic pattern of triangles (*cf.* Plate 49); the hieroglyphs of the name and titles have been cut out of sheet and soldered to the flat ground which has been inlaid with pieces of lapis lazuli cut roughly to shape and cemented on. This jewel has a somewhat crude and barbaric splendour which reflects the violent and war-like character of the age in which it was made. The internal diameter of the armlet (8·1 cm.) is greater than that of the other armlets of Queen Ah-hotpe, and suggests therefore that it was worn by Amosis himself, perhaps in his earlier years.

53 Necklace of three flies on a chain, gold. H. 9·0 cm. In the Cairo Museum, Cat. No. 52671.
The Order of the Golden Fly appears to have been a military decoration, perhaps of Canaanite origin (*cf.* Beelzebub, 'Lord of Flies') bestowed for valour in the field (see p. 19). These three examples found among Ah-hotpe's jewels are the largest and best versions of such an award which, in view of the amount of gold that went into their making, was of great intrinsic value. The design of the flies is of admirable boldness and simplicity. A flat base-plate of A-shape outlining the wings has had soldered to it a hemispheroidal shape representing the head with its large multiple eyes and thorax. This has been worked separately by hammering gold plate into a mould and chasing in the details. The stripes on the thorax have been simulated by cutting six longitudinal and two transverse slots. As the wearer moves the flash of light over this lattice of metal gives something of the iridescence of the natural insect. The flies are suspended by large rings soldered between the eyes on a loop-in-loop chain furnished with a simple hook-and-eye fastener.

54 Armlet, gold inlaid with carnelian, lapis lazuli and turquoise (?). D. 6·6 cm. H. 7·3 cm. In the Cairo Museum, Cat. No. 52068.
This is an early example of a kind of bracelet that, in the New Kingdom, was to supplement the flexible types which had been so characteristic of earlier times. In essence it consists of two rigid half-cylinders hinged to-gether at both ends, one hinge-pin being fixed and the other furnished with

a knob by which it can be withdrawn or inserted to form a fastening (*cf.* Plates 49, 57, 64, 129, 135). In this example one half is made in the form of Nekhebet, the vulture goddess of Upper Egypt holding *shen*-signs in her talons; and the other, as two curved bars inlaid with blue and green stones between thick gold cloisons and joined together at their centre by a gold disk inlaid with carnelian. From this boss a thick wire, square in section, runs left and right between the two bars to support a lotus bud at the junction with the hinge. The green inlays have discoloured to brown in places and other inlays are missing, notably the beak of the vulture. The design suggests that this bracelet was intended to be worn on the upper arm. The drawing of the bird is poor and the techniques show a considerable decline from the standards of the Middle Kingdom. The whole jewel has a somewhat rustic character more indicative of a provincial studio than a Memphite atelier. It may therefore date to the reign of Ka-mose. Its condition shows that it had suffered some damage in use.

55 Falcon Collar, gold with green and blue inlays. W. (of each terminal) 5·5 cm. In the Cairo Museum, Cat. No. 52672.

This collar has been reconstructed from a number of the elements found loose on the body of Ah-hotpe, but nearly one hundred and forty other pieces (Cat. No. 52733) have not been included. In view of the unique design of this jewel there is now no certainty about how it should be re-strung. As restored at present, the collar has fourteen rows of beads whereas the falcon headed shoulder pieces are perforated with eight holes. It is probable that around the mummy of the queen was originally fastened a ceremonial apron (*cf.* Plate 9), or at least a belt with a tail, and that parts of these have got mixed up with matching elements from her collar. It is also probable that many small ring beads in blue and green frit matching the colour of the inlays and keeping the various elements in position on the strings have been lost. The terminals were evidently made by hammering gold foil over a wood or stone positive and soldering each half shell to a flat plate before trimming the edges. Green and blue inlays, probably of thin frit, have been cemented into the cloisons. The lower edges have been perforated by the thread holes which run diagonally to emerge from the lower border of the back-plates. The various elements have been made by hammering gold foil into suitable moulds and trimming the edges. They include lions pursuing ibex, gazelles, scrolls, birds in flight, winged uraei and cats. While many of these designs are characteristically Egyptian, some of them suggest Aegean influence, particularly in such details as the 'flying gallop' of the coursing animals. At least the profusion and combination of such elements in a collar of traditional form is distinctly un-Egyptian and may represent the more Asiatic taste of the Hyksos rulers of Lower Egypt who were the patrons of the Memphite jewellers before the conquests of Amosis.

56 Pendant on a chain, gold and lapis lazuli. L. (of chain) 201 cm., H. (of scarab) 3·0 cm. In the Cairo Museum, Cat. No. 52670.

This jewel is technically the finest among Ah-hotpe's treasure and demonstrates that the Egyptian jeweller at this period was capable of work well able to hold its own with the best of the past. This may indicate that it was made in a Memphite workshop late in the reign of Amosis. The long chain is a sextuple loop-in-loop type made with great skill and regularity. It is fitted at its ends with two ferrules each in the form of a goose-head recurved on its elongated neck which is inscribed with one of the two great names of Amosis. At the back of the head is soldered a ring as a means of fastening the ends with a tie-cord. The scarab is made from two heavy gold plates, one forming the underpart and the other the back, this latter being fitted with cloisons to form seven horizontal cells on the pro-thorax and twelve on the elytra of the insect. These cells are fitted with pieces of lapis lazuli cut to size and cemented in position. The legs were cast separately and soldered to the base-plate giving the underside of the scarab a most naturalistic appearance. The two forelegs hold a ring, and a second ring is soldered to the rear legs. Through these rings passes a suspension in the form of a loop of twisted wire of a somewhat improvised nature; this may indicate that the scarab was not originally designed to be worn on this chain, but had been requisitioned for use as a heart scarab.

57 Bracelet, gold inlaid with lapis lazuli. Greater diam. 5·5 cm., smaller diam. 4·8 cm. In the Cairo Museum, Cat. No. 52069.

This is another example of the rigid bracelet (cf. Plate 54). It consists of two half cylinders to which have been soldered the various elements of the design cut in gold plate with the details added by chasing. The background to this raised scene has been inlaid with a mosaic of pieces of lapis lazuli cemented in position with a resinous adhesive which is visible as a black substance where the inlays are missing. The balanced scene on the right half shows, centre, a fan above a *shen*-sign, and left the Earth God Geb wearing a short cloak and the Lower Egyptian Crown as he supports his son, King Amosis, who kneels before him to be crowned. A complementary scene on the right shows Geb wearing the Crown of Upper Egypt. The names, titles and epithets of the king are given in two panels flanking the hinges at both ends. The other half-cylinder shows the 'Souls of Pe' and the 'Souls of Nekhen', the ancestral spirits of the Kings of Upper and Lower Egypt, as kneeling men wearing jackal or falcon masks and raising their arms in the *henu*-rite of jubilation to promise Amosis 'all joy' and 'all life and sovereignty for ever'. The two halves are fixed together by hinges, one pin of which is retractable to form the clasp. The theme of the decoration is the crowning of Amosis and his recognition as a descendant of all the divine Pharaohs. It is therefore probably part of his coronation regalia like the pectoral in Plate 50.

58 Bracelet, gold. D. (of opening) 6 cm. In the Cairo Museum, Cat. No. 52073.

This is one of only two known examples of a type of bracelet commonly shown on the monuments of the XVIIIth Dynasty (*cf.* Plates 116, 119) and which is probably a translation into metal of an ivory archetype. The jewel has been made by bending a strip of gold, 3·3 cm. in width, into a circle and soldering the two ends together. The resulting cylinder has been hammered on stakes so as to raise an expansion on the cylinder wall for most of its height leaving, however, an upper and lower border.

59 Circlet of a queen or princess, electrum. H. (of stag's head) 8·5 cm. From Salhiya (?) in the Eastern Delta. In the Metropolitan Museum, New York, Reg. No. 68.136.1

This unique crown, consisting of a band of electrum 1·5 cm. wide perforated to take tie-strings at the rear and mounted with rosettes and animal heads, appears to have been made in Egypt largely under Asiatic inspiration, if it is not an Asiatic import. In the XVIIIth Dynasty it became the fashion to decorate the diadems of princesses and lesser queens with the figure of a gazelle's head in place of the uraeus or vulture of principal queens (*cf.* Plates 60, 61). Thus Sit-Amun, the eldest daughter of Amenophis III, is shown wearing such an ornament attached to her fillet in a relief on the back of a chair which she contributed to her grandparent's burial furniture. In the North Syrian Kingdom of Ugarit a gazelle signified a young prince or princess; and this crown with its four gazelle heads may have been part of the trousseau of a foreign princess sent as a bride for one of the Pharaohs according to the diplomacy of the age. The four octafoil rosettes, too, are not specifically Egyptian with their sharply pointed petals, but they recall the eight-pointed star-shapes among the granular jewellery of Khnumet (*cf.* Plate 29, and also the parures found at Ur of 2500 BC). They raise, too, a faint echo of the Aegean in their resemblance to the applied flowers on a Middle Minoan krater of Kamares ware from Phaestos. The most extraordinary feature of the diadem, however, is the large hollow deer-head which decorates the centre of the band. Although the deer, under the name of *henen*, is sometimes represented in Egypt from Pre-dynastic times till the XIXth Dynasty, there is no positive evidence that the species was ever indigenous to Egypt or introduced there in ancient times except as stray marvels from Asia. In an inscription dated to regnal year 38 of Tuthmosis III, for instance, one stag is listed among the tribute brought from Asia. Many of the Egyptian pictures of deer were clearly made by artists who had never seen the actual animal. The stylized treatment of deer antlers on this diadem, in contrast to the horns of the gazelles, does not suggest the work of a craftsman who was familiar with the appearance of the stag. The nearest parallel to it in Egyptian art is to be sought in the horns of a deer painted in the Middle Kingdom tomb of Baket (No. 15) at Beni Hasan. For this reason the crown may well be the work of an Egyptian goldsmith and not an Asiatic import. It is reputed to have been found with other goldwork of the Middle Kingdom on a remote Delta site not far from the Hyksos stronghold of Avaris; and while the Metropolitan Museum authorities do not rule out a date for it in the late Middle Kingdom, they tend to regard it as of Hyksos origin, contemporary with the last of these rulers in Lower Egypt. If this is so, it is one of the very few pieces of Hyksos metalwork to have escaped the melting pot of the victorious Amosis.

60 Royal concubines, detail from a wall painting in tomb No. 69 of Menna at Western Thebes. After the copy by Nina de G. Davies in the British Museum. Middle XVIIIth Dynasty.

This portion of the painted tomb chapel shows two of the daughters of Menna who were subsidiary wives of Amenophis III. The proud Egyptian beauties are shown in all their finery which not only includes large gold earrings, collars, bracelets and armlets but a fillet tied round the brows with the ends falling behind. Beneath the fillet is a diadem carrying a gazelle head in front. The vertical rear plumes of Sit-Hathor-Yunet's circlet have here been transferred to the front of the head. The elaborate gold ornament on top of the hair is probably a receptacle for holding the cone of scented unguent which, as it melted, perfumed the wearer's hair and person. This representation should be compared with the following examples from actual parures of two generations earlier.

61–66 If the treasure of Queen Ah-hotpe is a sampling of the craft of the Egyptian jewellers at the very beginning of the XVIIIth Dynasty, the treasure of the three queens of Tuthmosis III, examples of which are shown in the next six plates, exhibits their skill a century later when Egypt was in full contact with the high culture of the Eastern Mediterranean and playing a cardinal role in it. The designs are more sophisticated, the techniques less fumbling, though the actual workmanship does not display the standards achieved in the Lahun and Dahshur jewels. This may be because it was made for secondary queens, evidently of Syrian or Canaanite origin to judge by their names, who were buried together in a small rock-cut tomb in a wady about two miles west of the Valley of the Kings at Western Thebes where their lord was laid to rest. The tomb was discovered in 1916 by natives of Qurna (see p. 8) who ransacked it for valuables which they sold to various dealers. The bulk of the plunder has been bought over the years by the Metropolitan Museum of New York where ingenious attempts have been made to restore it to its former appearance. The tomb had been subject to periodical flooding and most of such materials as faience, frit and wood had rotted away. Careless handling by the plunderers resulted in further losses, and copies made by forgers of some of the gold elements before they were sold to dealers has increased the confusion. Originally, however, each queen seems to have been provided with a full set of ornaments as well as toilet articles and tableware of considerable value.

61 Circlet, gold, inlaid with carnelian, blue and green frit (now decayed). L. (of diadem) 43 cm. In New York, M.M.A. Reg. No. 26.8.99.
The circlet is a variation on the classical fillet worn from earliest times (*cf.* Plates 4, 39). A departure from such designs is a sagittal band that prevents the diadem from slipping over the face (*cf.* Plate 123). The bands are joined in a T-shape which tapers from 2·8 cm. at their junction to 1·6 cm. at their ends. These are furnished with leopard heads (*cf.* Plate 36) worked separately and soldered in place holding rings in their mouths through which tie-cords are passed. Both bands are decorated with simplified rosettes of twelve petals, probably representing marguerites rather than the traditional papyrus and lotus flowers of earlier circlets, set in circular gold frames soldered in position—two on the sagittal band and four on the fillet. Only the carnelian inlays have survived; the other inlays have been reduced by centuries of damp to the condition of a discoloured paste. The special feature of this head-dress, however, is the pair of gazelle heads which appear to have been made by beating heavy gold foil over a stone or wood positive; joining the two half-shells longitudinally and soldering on the horns worked separately. They are detachable, fitting onto curved thimbles soldered to the front of the diadem. Below them originally hung a pendant from the seven little rings, perhaps either a lotus flower and buds, or a bead tassel similar to those shown in Plates 121 and 122. The triple necklaces shown in this illustration, and in Plate 62, have been made up from the great mass of lenticular beads in blue faience that were recovered from this deposit.

62 The 'Long' Head-dress, gold inlaid with carnelian, turquoise and coloured frit (now decayed). H. 37 cm. In New York, M.M.A. Reg. No. 26.8.117.
This wig, or hair-cover, is a development of the rosette decorations sewn or strung to the braided tresses of the wearer (*cf.* Plates 6, 23). In this example, the rosettes are more numerous and elaborate and are strung on a support which is independent of the hair. A considerable number of graduated cloisonné elements, each consisting of a twelve-rayed rosette with two upper corner-pieces, were recovered from the debris in the tomb and some of these have found their way into various collections. But the majority of them have been acquired by the Metropolitan Museum and reveal that two if not three head-dresses of this kind were originally deposited with the burials. The reconstruction here illustrated is of about 850 inlaid pieces strung in such a way as to form a flexible golden cowl descending at the back and front to cover the typical long wig or coiffure of Egyptian women (*cf.* Plate 127). The warrant for this reconstruction is the fortunate survival of a some-

what well-worn, oval, crown-plate consisting of two sheets of gold kept apart by borders and cross ribs. The upper plate is decorated with a chased palm-tree design in which gold leaves alternate with inlaid leaves, but the inlay has decayed and is now missing. Around the periphery of the plate are soldered over thirty gold rings from which hang the rosettes on two strings by means of small gold tubes soldered to their sides, interlocking with others on adjacent strings and separated by gold ring-beads. The summit of each vertical section ends in a lozenge made in one piece with the first rosette; and the bottom fringe is composed of a triple lunette similarly made in a unit with the last rosette. The front of the crown-plate may also have carried a fringe of pendant tassels (*cf.* Plate 61). Originally the rosettes were inlaid with blue and green artificial stones which have decayed through damp to the condition of a white paste, but which have been identified as glass. Increasing skill and success were being achieved at this period in the manufacture of objects in coloured glass; and indeed the possessions of the three queens included at least two glass goblets in a good state of preservation. In view of their survival, it is doubtful whether the inlays were of glass, and they are more likely to have been of faience or frit ('Egyptian blue', see pp. 35–36). This head-dress, when it first left the hands of the jeweller, must have been a glittering and opulent object, particularly in the Egyptian sunshine; but it was also a heavy one and its present weight of over one kilogram will have to be doubled to arrive at some idea of how much it weighed when all its inlays were in place.

63   *Upper:* A belt of gold, carnelian, turquoise and blue faience (?) beads. L. *c.* 78 cm. In New York, M.M.A. Reg. No. 26.8.118–9.
The classical Egyptian garment worn by women was the simple linen shift held up by shoulder-straps (*cf* Plate 32). No belt was required for this, though girdles might be worn beneath it (*cf.* Plate 67). In the later years of the XVIIIth Dynasty the more flowing robes of the time demanded some kind of sash to confine the gown around the waist, and a long ribbed girdle usually woven of some red material, makes its appearance (*cf.* Plate 127). The two examples in the Metropolitan Museum, however, are the only examples known of a woman's belt in Ancient Egypt. It consists of a number of coloured stone beads shaped like acacia seeds (*cf.* Plate 35) strung between spacer-bars consisting of seven similarly shaped gold beads soldered together. The end-pieces (not illustrated) consist of two hollow boxes of the same height as the spacers (11 cm.) having rings which intermesh with each other when the two parts are brought together and locked by inserting a pin (*cf.* Plate 49).

Lower: A girdle, gold and red glass. L. 96 cm. In New York, M.M.A. Reg. No. 26.8.41.
This jewel was worn under the gown (*cf.* Plate 67). It follows the design of

such girdles in the New Kingdom, but for the semi-circular main beads (see Plate 48), it substitutes twenty-two hollow gold fishes, each made in two half-shells and soldered along their seams with perforations to take three strings of gold and red glass beads. Like all such girdles it is a continuous zone without a clasp and was put on by passing it over the head and shoulders and allowing it to rest on the hips.

64 Bracelets, gold inlaid with carnelian, turquoise and blue frit (?). L. 6·0 cm., D. *c.* 5·6 cm. tapering to 5·3 cm. In New York, M.M.A. Reg. No.26.8.125–8. These are two of the three pairs of bracelets of this type which were owned by the queens. They are of rigid pattern with pin fastenings (*cf.* Plate 57). The exteriors are fashioned by the cloisonné technique with rims and raised gold bars alternating with cells of equal width for the insertion of plaques of carnelian, turquoise and a blue substance, now decayed, which was probably a blue frit imitating lapis lazuli ('Egyptian blue' see p. 36). These inlays are ribbed to imitate fifteen rows of cylindrical beads strung between gold spacers. The insides of the bracelets are inscribed with the names and titles of Tuthmosis III and show signs of wear. The three queens also had armlets and anklets of other designs (see Plates 84 and 85).

65 Falcon Collar, gold inlaid with carnelian, turquoise and blue and green frit (decayed). Size of terminals. W. 7·4 cm., H. 5·2 cm. In New York, M.M.A. Reg. No. 26.8.59 *et. al.*
The collar has been reconstructed from the two shoulder-pieces in the form of falcon heads, with eyes inlaid with obsidian and markings in carnelian and turquoise (?), the latter somewhat discoloured, and with beads that have been selected in modern times because of the same colour relationships and standard of craftsmanship. The order of stringing is somewhat uncertain and it is possible that elements from two collars have been combined here. The falcon head terminals have the inlaid details indicated on the reverse by chasing and are inscribed with the title and prenomen of Tuthmosis III. Their lower edge is perforated with eight thread holes suggesting that the collars for which they were designed comprised seven rows of captive beads and a possible further row of freely hanging pendants. The tie-strings have been restored.

66 Broad Collar, gold inlaid with carnelian, turquoise and blue frit (decayed). Size of terminals, W. 7·2 cm., H. 3·5 cm. In New York, M.M.A. Reg. No. 26.8.135, 70 *et. al.*
This collar is also restored, the basis for the reconstruction being the two shoulder-pieces with a design of the king's prenomen, centre, flanked by two lotus flowers in cloisonné-work inlaid with carnelian, turquoise and blue frit, of which little now remains. The beads were in the form of *nefer*-signs in gold, graduated in size, half inlaid with coloured stones or frit

(mostly missing), and half with plain gold fronts, showing that the gold *nefers* alternated with coloured ones. In the re-stringing, the plain gold backs of the *nefers* and the palmette pendants have been shown with the inlaid fronts of the shoulder pieces to give a uniform appearance. With this reconstruction has been included a lotus flower counterpoise still retaining some of its carnelian and turquoise inlays. It would probably have had a lower border of bead tassels (*cf.* Plate 101).

67 Orchestra and dancers, part of a wall painting from the tomb of Neb-amun in the British Museum. Reign of Amenophis III, XVIIIth Dynasty.

The complete scene shows guests being entertained at a banquet. The squatting girls play on the double pipes, clap their hands and sing of the joys of the Inundation, when 'the whole land is flooded with love', while two of their number perform a posturing dance. Their jewellery is worthy of note. All wear fillets on their heads, probably made of strips of papyrus sewn with leaves and flower petals (*cf.* Plate 113), or bead versions of such an ornament. A similar decoration surrounds the container holding the unguent cone on top of their hair (*cf.* Plate 60). A lotus flower tucked in the fillet hangs over the forehead. Around their necks they wear festal collars of the kind illustrated in Plate 113, and over them plain gold collars of the type shown in Plate 66, or complete inlaid gold and silver versions of the floral collar. Their ear-rings or ear-plugs are large (*cf.* Plate 68). They wear two or three gold bracelets on each forearm and two gold inlaid armlets. In addition, because the dancers have divested themselves of their gowns, the girdles around their hips (*cf.* Plates 48, 63) are readily visible.

68 Ear ornaments, gold, faience, glass and stone, XVIII–XXth Dynasties. In the Royal Scottish Museum, Edinburgh.

Top Row: Ear-plugs in faience and gold (Reg. Nos. 1965.354, 1883.49.12, 1965. 355). The two outer specimens (diam. 4, and 3·2 cm.) are made of faience and have a groove round the periphery by which they could be retained in a hole stretched in the ear-lobe. The outer face is domed and the decoration recalls the different designs on the ear-plugs shown in Plate 67. These objects were formerly thought to be bobbins for holding thread wound in the peripheral channel; but similar examples in wood and ivory are still used in parts of East Africa, and the distended holes in the ear-lobes of some mummies of women at this period leave little doubt about what their real purpose was. The specimen in the middle (diam. 4 cm.) is made of massive gold and was found in the vicinity of the Royal Tomb at Amarna. It is decorated with granular work, twisted wires, made by the block twisting process (see p. 86), and a border of running spirals of plain wire (*cf.* Plate 122). Since it would stretch the hole in the ear-lobe to a diameter of 1·5 cm. to retain it in position, it probably belonged to a woman of mature years, perhaps Queen Nefert-iti or Queen Tiye.

Middle Row: Ear-rings in glass and jasper. From the Acworth Collection. Average diam. 2·5 cm. Reg. Nos. 1961.514, 516–8, 528.

Four of the ear-rings here illustrated are made of canes of glass of two colours bent into a penannular shape and formed with a loop at each end. A stud of metal, wood or ivory was passed through these stirrups and a hole in the lobe of the ear to hold them in position. This was a type of ear-ring which was evidently worn by children and sometimes by men: Kha, for instance, has a large pair in gold on his mummy, still in its wrappings, at Turin (*cf.* Plate 117). The centre ring is made of red jasper of D-section and is provided with a perforated lug from which hang two bead tassels. The position of the slit shows how these rings were worn. They were inserted by stretching the lobe to a very thin ribbon of flesh to pass through the gap. It may be assumed that, once in position, the rings were removed very infrequently, if at all.

Bottom Row: Ear-studs in gold, faience and stone. Average diam. 2·5 cm., average length, 3·2 cm. (Reg. Nos. 1883.49, 9, 10; 1965.350–2).

These little mushroom-shaped studs appear about the Amarna Period. Three of those illustrated here are made of faience in two or more colours with that high degree of skill which is characteristic of the products of the glass and faience workers during this period. The white stone specimen is of the same date. The two outer specimens of gold came from the Royal Tomb at Amarna and probably belonged to one of the royal daughters or wives.

69 Finger-rings, gold and carnelian, reign of Akhenaten. In the Royal Scottish Museum, Edinburgh. Reg. Nos. 1883.49.8,2,1; 190.1.

All the rings with the exception of the specimen on the right were found in the vicinity of the Royal Tomb at Amarna and were doubtless part of the furnishings pilfered and cached nearby during the removal of the burials to Thebes in the reign of Tut-ankh-amun. The two examples on the left have a swivelling bezel which is threaded on the ring by drawing out the ends of the loop into very long wires, passing them through its longitudinal hole from opposite ends, and coiling them onto the body. The first ring (diam. 2·3 cm.) has a bezel in the form of a carnelian *wedjet*-eye with a *sa*-sign engraved on its reverse. The second (diam. 3 cm.) has a bezel of gold surmounted by the figure of a frog and encircled by a double row of large granules. The underside is inscribed with the name of the goddess Mut and the title, 'Lady of Heaven'. The two rings on the right are examples of the massive signet rings of the period made by casting in *cire perdue*, the bezel being *en masse* with the hoop. The inscription, in intaglio, was also cut in the wax before the ring was fitted with a sprue and invested with fine clay. All that remained to do after casting was to remove the surplus metal and polish up the surface. The gold ring (diam. 2·5 cm.) is inscribed with the name of Queen Nefert-iti: the other specimen (diam. 2 cm.) is made of an alloy of gold with a high copper content (see p. 31), peculiar to this period. It bears the prenomen of 'The Good God Akhenaten' in a cartouche upon a bark with prow and stern in the form of a royal head wearing horns and plumes.

70 Three finger-rings, gold and silver. L. (of bezels) 2·5, 2·1, 2·5 cm. Amarna Period, XVIIIth Dynasty. In the private collection of Dr K. J. Stern, London. These signet rings were made by the same technique as the preceding pair. The first is a massive specimen cast in silver of great purity and inscribed with a version of the prenomen of Amenophis III who is also described as 'the Son of Amun' and 'Happy in Wealth'. The gold ring is inscribed with the phrase, 'Aten, dwelling on the horizon, is the lord of joy'. The third example, (formerly in the Macgregor Collection) is also in silver of high quality and is inscribed with the prenomen of Akhenaten (Nefer-kheperu-re Wa-en-re) and the epithet, 'Beloved of Re-Herakhty'.

71 Broad Collar of King Smenkh-ka-re, gold and electrum inlaid with coloured glass. Size of terminals, L. 9 cm., H. 4·5 cm. Found on the body of the king in tomb No. 55 in the Valley of the Kings in 1907. In the Cairo Museum, Cat. No. 52, 674.
The collar is shown in the condition in which it was re-threaded soon after its recovery from the tomb but, owing to the lack of any records kept by the excavators, Davis and Ayrton, it is impossible to say how authentic the reconstruction is. The collar is obviously incomplete, a considerable number of ring beads are missing from the six strings, and other elements were retrieved which are not included; a few parts were stolen by Davis' men. Since each shoulder-piece is perforated with six holes there were five rows of pendants which are present here; but in a confusion of sizes and sequences. For an idea of its proper appearance see the faience version in Plate 125. The terminals are made in the form of hollow perforated bars to which are soldered lotus flowers inlaid with coloured glass, most of which is missing. The first row is made of plaques, each consisting of a leaf-shape with its side-piece attached, forming a rhomboidal unit. These have ring-beads soldered at the top and bottom and are inlaid with coloured glass. The other pendants in the form of date-shapes, *nefers*, and drop-beads, are made of thin electrum beaten into moulds of graduated sizes, soldered to a back-plate and fitted with rings at both extremities.

72 Vulture Collar of King Smenkh-ka-re, gold. H. 24 cm., W. 21 cm. Found on the head of the king in tomb No. 55 in the Valley of the Kings in 1907. In the Cairo Museum, Cat. No. 52, 643.
This is a rare example of the 'Collar of the Vulture' known from the coffin pictures of the Middle Kingdom. It had suffered some damage before

it was put in the position in which it was found, having lost its right talon holding a *shen*-sign and the *menkhet* counterpoise on a gold wire that connected the two perforated lugs near the tips of the wings (*cf.* Plate 111). A repair had also been made by soldering a patch onto the right pinion. The vulture is cut in thick sheet gold, the lower edges of the design being turned up for a millimetre to give the figure stability. The outline and feathering of the bird is most expertly indicated by unfaltering lines incised by chasing. This collar, and the somewhat inferior specimen found on the body of Tut-ankh-amun, are the only surviving examples of a funerary jewel with which all the mummies of the great Pharaohs were once provided. A more elaborate version in flexible cloisonné-work was also found upon Tut-ankh-amun (see Plate 111).

73 First pectoral of Sit-Hathor-Yunet. Reverse of the jewel illustrated in Plate 37, showing the chasing of the gold back.
'It has been said that the pectoral was conceived to be viewed usually from a respectful distance. Yet it will bear the most intimately close inspection, and the repetition of the details of the design wrought and chased on its back is as marvellously executed as its gaily coloured front. In fact, the subtlely modelled reverse, with each detail moulded and chased with microscopic accuracy, is perhaps even more wonderful than the obverse'. H. E. Winlock.

74 Second pectoral of Sit-Hathor-Yunet. Reverse of the jewel illustrated in Plate 38, showing the chasing of the gold back.
'The deterioration of the goldsmith's work is obvious, and the backs of the two pectorals show this most strikingly. The outline of the second lacks the airy lightness of the first pectoral; the details are clumsy; the subtle, low relief has been flattened out, and the chasing is heavy and stumbling in comparison with the work of (the earlier) jeweller.' H. E. Winlock.

75 Bracelets of Sit-Hathor-Yunet, a pair, shown clasped. For particulars see Plate 40.
The bracelets worn on the wrist were too long and close-fitting to allow for one end to be clipped into the other in the same way as the anklets could be manipulated (*cf.* Fig. 34). Instead, a separate detachable slide connected the two ends and with its inscription in coloured frits against a carnelian ground, giving the titles and prenomen of Ammenemes III, formed an element in the alternating green and red stripes of the beadwork. So that the two slides should not be confused their tongues and grooves were marked with different notches.

76 Pectoral of Queen Mereret. Reverse of the jewel illustrated in Plate 42, showing the chasing of the gold back.
The details of the composition are shown more clearly in the reverse than

the obverse, but the general fussiness and illogicality of the design with the inscriptions acting as supports and space-fillers are only too apparent.

77 Fish pendant, gold inlaid with carnelian, turquoise and lapis lazuli. L. 4 cm. Middle XIIth Dynasty. In the Walters Art Gallery, Baltimore. Reg. No. 57.1072.

78 Fish pendant, gold. L. 4 cm. Excavated at Haraga. Middle XIIth Dynasty. In the Royal Scottish Museum, Edinburgh. Reg. No. 1914.1079.
The fish may have been a charm against drowning and was worn suspended from the hair, probably by a few strands which passed through the ring at the mouth (cf. Fig 22). The lower specimen, however, was the largest in a set of five fish pendants found worn around the neck of an infant. It is made by working heavy gold foil around a suitable positive, trimming the two half-shells and filling them with a fine clay, inserting fins and tail along the medial line and soldering the two halves by a colloidal process. Despite its relatively small size, the workmanship is exquisite, and the illustration has been enlarged without any detriment. The upper specimen of similar date and size was inlaid with hard stones most of which have now disappeared.

79–81 Jewellery excavated from the shaft of tomb No. 124 at Rikka in 1913. Gold inlaid with carnelian, lapis lazuli and turquoise. Middle XIIth Dynasty. In the Manchester Museum, Reg. Nos. 5968, 5966.
The fact that the owner's valuable jewellery was found virtually intact in his tomb is due to a macabre circumstance. The excavators found that the roof of the burial chamber had collapsed upon both the rightful occupant and an intruder while the latter was in the act of despoiling the mummy. His accomplices, who were evidently the necropolis guards, hastily filled up the hole they had dug, leaving their dead confederate still clutching his victim, and so obscured all traces of the crime for nearly four thousand years. The pectoral was found on the breast of the mummy a little below the gold shell (Plate 79), and a second broken pectoral with a design incorporating the name of Sesostris II.
The gold bivalve shell (H. 2·2 cm.) has a suspension ring soldered at the point of the hinge (cf. Plate 45) and the prenomen of Sesostris III in gold wire soldered to its body. The cartouche is supported by a uraeus on either side, a design which is not uncommon at this period.
The cloisonné-work pectoral (H. 3·8 cm., W. 4·5 cm.) resembles the Eton College specimen in its general design (cf. Plates 25, 26) and workmanship. The shrine consists of a base-bar inlaid with a block border from which springs a papyrus rush at each end to support the left and right wedjet-eyes of Horus with the sun-disk between them. A nehbet-sceptre forms the central element and on either side of it is a bird upon the nub-glyph for a

collar. This is evidently a play upon the symbol of the falcon perched upon the *nub*-sign, as representing Horus, incarnate in the king, triumphant over evil (*cf.* Plate 33). In place of the falcons, however, appear other birds, perhaps the ubiquitous Egyptian crow.

82, 83　Circlet of King Intef (Nub-kheper-re), gold, silver and coloured glass. D. 18 cm. XVIIth Dynasty. In the Rijksmuseum, Leyden. Reg. No. AO. 11a. This is an example of a crown made in the form of a boatman's circlet at a somewhat impoverished period in Ancient Egyptian history. The burial of Nub-kheper-re was found by the Arabs in the Dira Abu l'Naga at Western Thebes in 1827, and the contents were dispersed among several collectors to find their way eventually into different museums in Europe. The coffin of the king is in the British Museum. The diadem which is illustrated here is reported to have been found upon the king's head outside the mummy bandages. With it was evidently found a disintegrated Broad Collar of faience ring beads and silver drop beads inlaid with light blue, green and dark blue glass, for these had arbitrarily been attached to the circlet by the Arabs before they disposed of it to the Chevalier d'Anastasi. From his collection it passed to Leyden. The circlet in its present condition consists of a band of silver decorated with a block border by chasing. To the front is attached a gold uraeus of somewhat crude manufacture. At the back is the usual bow-knot in the form of a disk of blue glass flanked by two lotus flowers made in cloisonné-work. Two short extensions of the band at the back simulate the ends of the tie; and two longer pendants represent streamers.

84–86　Jewellery from the burial of the three queens of Tuthmosis III. XVIIIth Dynasty. In the Metropolitan Museum of Art, New York. For details of the find see Plates 61–66.

84　Armlet, gold, carnelian, 'Egyptian blue (?)' and green felspar. L. 24 cm., W. 5·2 cm. M.M.A. Reg. No. 26.8.121.
　　This ornament is probably a bracelet for wearing on the upper arm and is a development of the lion armlets of the Dahshur and Lahun princesses and King Kamose, and of the sphinx armlet of Amosis (*cf.* Plates 51, 52). In the XVIIth Dynasty, Queen Sobek-em-saf wore a similar armlet adorned with cats recumbent upon the spacer bars and these latter are now in the British Museum (Reg. Nos. 57699–700). The three queens of Tuthmosis III each seem to have had a pair of armlets, one of which has been reconstructed here from different elements. The central feature is a gold bar in the form of a shallow box perforated with fifteen holes in its long sides through which the threads pass. On its upper surface were originally five recumbent cats, their fore-paws crossed and their heads turned to the right. In the corresponding armlet of the pair their heads are turned to the left. The two cast gold cats

are soldered in position. The central cat in the group carved in carnelian is pinched into a gold frame soldered to the bar. The two empty mounts once held cats in 'Egyptian blue' or faience to complete the colour scheme but these have decayed with damp and have disappeared. The beads are gold, carnelian and green felspar barrels. Apart from two lapis lazuli beads the blue elements have disintegrated and are here restored. The gold barrels are soldered in columns of fifteen to form spacer bars. The clasps are similar in action to those in Plate 49, being fixed with a pin.

85   Anklets, a pair, gold. D. 5·4 cm. M.M.A. Reg. No. 26.8.133–4.
Each anklet consists of two short half-cylinders hinged together. The retractable pin forming the clasp may be seen in position in the left hinge of the right-hand specimen. They are made of sheet metal, the rims being thickened to give strength and rigidity, and are inscribed with the names of Tuthmosis III chased on the inner surface. As they show little signs of wear they have been considered as destined only for funerary use. It is difficult to accept this in the case of another pair which has been inscribed with the name of the co-regent, Queen Hatshepsut, on the outer surfaces.

86   Necklaces, gold and silver. M.M.A. Reg. Nos. 21.6.1; 26.8.62, 209, 210, 208, 65, 64; 205.
A selection of some of the beads recovered from the deposit are shown in this plate, arbitrarily strung. From the top downwards they are:
1 A long string of gold beads each consisting of five grains soldered around a central hole which when threaded together intermesh to form a long flexible tube of gold.
2, 3 Two strings of ring beads separating nineteen and twenty falcons, each 1·6 cm. high, wearing the Double Crown. Each is formed by beating gold foil into a suitable mould and soldering on a backplate perforated with an air-hole. A suspension ring is soldered on the reverse.
4 A similar necklace but composed of figures of the hippopotamus goddess Toweris, 1 cm. high.
5 Sixteen plaques (1·6 × 1·4 cm.) made in the shape of a shrine with a striated tubular cornice by hammering gold sheet into a mould incised with the squatting figure of the goddess Maet.
6 Thirty-three flies (*cf.* Plate 53) each 1·4 cm. long formed by beating out the front in a suitable die and soldering it to a back-plate perforated with an air-hole. A suspension ring is soldered between the eyes and the pendants so formed have been threaded between ring and barrel beads.
7 A necklace of seventy-one blackened silver and thirteen green quartz beads 0·4 to 0·6 cm. in diameter. The metal beads are formed of a composition of a resinous nature to which two thin silver hemispherical caps have been fitted by heating.

87–89   Jewels of Amenophis III. Three carved hardstone bracelet plaques in modern gold settings. Average length 5 cm. In the Metropolitan Museum of Art, New York, Reg. Nos. 26.7.1339, 40, 42.

In all, five hardstone plaques are known from bracelets which were made for Amenophis III on the occasion of one of his jubilees, probably the first. For some idea of their appearance when complete, see the fifth bracelet from the top in each row of the Tut-ankh-amun specimens in Plate 112. One fragment in New York shows the king kneeling to be crowned by Re-Herakhty. A complete specimen, also in New York, shows the diminutive figure of a fan-bearer bowing deferentially in the royal presence and is a reminder that jewels of this character were given by high officials to the kings they served on such important events as coronations and jubilees (*cf.* Figs. 7 and 8). The three most celebrated of these plaques, however, are the trio that were formerly in the Carnarvon Collection and are believed to have been discovered in a dump of rubbish in the vicinity of the tomb of Amenophis III at Thebes. Both the front and back surfaces have been curved to fit the contours of the arm they were meant to embellish.

87   A dark sard plaque carved *à jour* showing a winged female sphinx, wearing bracelets and a cap surmounted by a plant motif, supporting the prenomen of Amenophis III. This may represent the lion goddess Tefnut who accepts the king's name in certain coronation scenes.

88   A carnelian plaque carved in relief with figures of Amenophis III and his chief queen Tiye seated in the jubilee palanquin and receiving emblems of long life and rule from two of their daughters, who worship them by shaking their sistra. This is the finest in the series, the crisp detail in the carving of the hard stone being exquisite.

89   A carnelian plaque carved in relief with figures of the king wearing jubilee garb and seated in the twin Pavilions of the Festival. He receives the emblems of long life and rule from the tall figure of Tiye impersonating a goddess.

90   Bracelet, bright blue faience. Outer diam. 8·5 cm. Partly restored. Reign of Amenophis III, XVIIIth Dynasty. In the Metropolitan Museum of Art, New York, Reg. No. 11.215.509.

This bracelet is an elaborate example of the costume jewellery that was made of faience in the reign of Amenophis III and his immediate successors. It is thought that such fragile, mass-produced jewels were distributed as favours on the occasions of festivals and state-banquets. The most common of such pieces are the many finger-rings which have been found, mostly in a fragmentary condition, on the ancient sites at Western Thebes, Amarna and Ghurab. For the most part they are faience versions of metal prototypes, in one or more colours. This bracelet, unfortunately incomplete, is a large and unique version of such ornaments, being in effect a greatly enlarged finger-ring with the bezel worked with the king's prenomen *à jour* instead of in relief.

91–112,   Jewellery from the tomb of King Tut-ankh-amun (*c.* 1362–1353 BC) now in
121–124   the Cairo Museum (see also Plates 153–156).

91   Finger rings of King Tut-ankh-amun, gold inlaid with coloured glass. Average diam. 2·0 cm. Late XVIIIth Dynasty. In the Cairo Museum. Carter Cat. Nos. (from top to bottom and left to right) 44E.G.F; D,I; J,H,C.

The group of rings here illustrated were found together tied in one of the king's scarves in an inlaid gilded chest where they had been stowed by the officials who cleared up the tomb after it had been violated by thieves. It would appear that the rings were recovered still wrapped in a purloined scarf before they could be carried off by the thieves. One, however, of the rings had had its hoop sundered from its bezel and only the latter (No. 44J) was retrieved.

All the rings are developments of the heavy signet rings shown in Plate 70, but they differ from them in having double or tripartite hoops (with the exception of Nos. 44F and G). In the case of 44E, D, and C these hoops end in floral capitals inlaid with coloured glass and finished with decorative lashings of gold wire. Nearly all the rings have bezels in single or double cartouche form enclosing rebuses on the king's name or figures of gods in low relief, the ground reserved in blue or lilac coloured glass which is virtually enamel. In rings 44D, I and J, the bezels are particularly elaborate. 44D has a lapis lazuli scarab, centre, carrying the moon disk and crescent in electrum flanked by two scarabs in gold surmounted by the sun-disk. On 44I there is a lapis lazuli scarab carrying a triple Atefu-crown protected front and rear by a moon-bark and a hovering falcon wearing the sun-disk. The most complicated of all the bezels is 44J, a masterpiece of miniature casting representing the worship of the sun-god. Re, as a falcon-headed man seated on a throne, is worshipped by the king (?) who kneels before him, flanked on either side by a squatting ape bearing the moon-disk and crescent and raising hands in praise. The whole scene is protected by the encircling wings of the crowned vulture Nekhebet of Upper Egypt and the falcon Horus of Lower Egypt.

92–101   A series of pectoral ornaments, all with the exception of Plates 99, 100 and 101 found within the Anubis Pylon in the 'Treasury' of the tomb (see Plate 154). They are funerary jewels based upon the idea of the transfiguration of the dead king within the primeval shrine or kiosk in which the demiurge first manifested himself at the creation of the world.

92   Pectoral, gold, inlaid with carnelian, red, light blue and dark blue glass, the

last somewhat decayed. H. 12·1 cm., W. 17·2 cm. Carter Cat. No. 261, P3. The kiosk is of simple form with a 'block border' base and supports, a cavetto cornice and a floral frieze. Within it is displayed the sky-goddess Nut in the form of a vulture with protective wings, tail outspread and talons clutching *shen*-signs. Between the bird and the frieze are the titles and names of the king and the name of the goddess. The design symbolizes the idea expressed in a funerary prayer found on coffins of the period: 'O my mother Nut, spread thyself over me and place me among the imperishable stars that are in thee, so that I die not.' The anchorage at each end of the cornice is perforated to take a necklace of three strings.

93 Pectoral, gold inlaid with carnelian, green, red, light blue and dark blue glass. H. 10·5 cm., W. 14·5 cm. Carter Cat. No. 261, J.
The kiosk is of slightly more elaborate form having in addition to its floral frieze a base of poppy-flowers and lotus buds. In the kiosk appears a scarab carved in the round in green felspar, its wings being of cloisonné-work. The disk of the new-born sun which it supports on its head is here elongated into an oval cartouche containing the prenomen of the king with the additional epithet, 'the Image of the Sun-god.' The design represents the daily resurrection at dawn of the sun-god with whom the king is identified. The anchorages at both ends of the cornice are worked to take two suspensory strings with plaquettes.

94 Pectoral, gold, inlaid with rock crystal backed with coloured cement, green, red, light blue and dark blue glass. H. 12·8 cm., W. 18·2 cm. Carter Cat. No. 261, N.
Within the kiosk is a large, bluish-grey, glazed stone (steatite?) scarab supported by kneeling figures of Isis (right) and Nephthys (left) as representatives of the guardian goddesses of the four quarters. The scarab representing the sun-god Khepri at dawn rolls the disk of the sun across the heavens. Here the disk is encircled by two uraei, symbolizing the king of Upper and Lower Egypt whose two great names appear surmounted by sun-disks between the forearms of the goddesses and the architrave. The design, like that of Plate 93, represents the daily re-birth of the king as the sun-god. Originally it was suspended on a necklace of three strings.

95 Pectoral, poor quality gold, inlaid with quartz set in red cement, green, red, light blue and dark blue glass, the last greatly decayed. H. 12 cm., W. 16·3 cm. Carter Cat. No. 261, I.
The kiosk is of simple form with a frieze of flower petals below the architrave which carries two anchorages, worked on each face with a winged protective serpent, to take a necklace of four strings. Within the kiosk the sun-god is seen appearing on the primeval *Djed*-column above the waters of Chaos, and is supported on either side by the goddesses Isis (right) and

Nephthys (left) with the wings of kites, representing two of the deities of the four quarters of the universe. Uraei wearing the White Crown of Upper Egypt (right) and the Red Crown of Lower Egypt (left) support the king's two 'great' names. The design symbolizes the original creation of the universe by the sun-god to whom the dead king has become assimilated.

96 Pectoral, poor quality gold, much tarnished, inlaid with carnelian (?), red, light blue and dark blue glass, the last badly deteriorated. H. 15·5 cm., W. 20 cm. Carter Cat. No. 261, O.

Within the primeval shrine, the cornice of which is flanked with a uraeus wearing a sun-disk on either side, appear the 'Two Ladies', Edjo the goddess of Lower Egypt (right) as a winged uraeus, wearing the Red Crown, and Nekhebet the goddess of Upper Egypt (left) as a vulture wearing the White Crown with flanking plumes. Both are resting on *neb*-baskets and protect with their wings the king who is shown mummiform wearing the *Atefu*-crown of coronation and jubilee, and holding sceptres. The label behind him giving his titles shows that he has now become assimilated to Osiris the god of Resurrection. *Shen*-signs symbolizing all the dominions ruled over by the king connect him to the two goddesses. Brief labels behind the goddesses show that they are also identified with Isis and Nephthys. The design symbolizes the resurrection of the dead king, ruler of Upper and Lower Egypt and all that the sun encircles, within the primeval shrine, fanned into life by the wings of Isis and Nephthys.

97 Pectoral, gold, inlaid with carnelian, red, light blue and dark blue glass. H. 12·6 cm., W. 14·3 cm. Carter Cat. No. 261, P1.

The kiosk is of simple form, the architrave below the cavetto cornice being decorated with a block border. Within it stands the sky goddess Nut as a woman with vulture's wings, described as 'the Great Spirit', her arms outspread in a protective gesture. Above her are the names and titles of the king. Below is a text to the effect that Nut stretches her arms over the dead king in order to protect his limbs. The cartouche of the king, however, shows traces of the name of Akhenaten beneath it, indicating that it was probably made early in the reign of that king and not used for his burial. The attachments for the strings at the side show that this jewel was meant to be worn as the central element in a belt or girdle consisting of four strands threaded with beads or plaques.

98 Pectoral, gold, inlaid with carnelian, dark red, light and dark blue glass. H. 16·5 cm., W. 24·4 cm. Carter Cat. No. 261, M. From the Anubis pylon (see Plate 154).

The base and supports of the kiosk are decorated with a block border, but in place of the usual cornice appears the winged disk of Horus of Edfu flanked by coiled uraei enfolding sun-disks. Within the kiosk are squatting figures of Isis (right) and Nephthys (left), representing two of the four quarters of the universe, and supporting the winged scarab of the sun-god in his aspect of Khepri at dawn (*cf.* Plates 93, 94). The scarab is carved in the round from a greenish speckled stone, on the flat reverse of which is inscribed a spell from the *Book of the Dead* exhorting the heart of the deceased not to bear false witness at the Last Judgement. The inlaid inscriptions linking the various parts give the names of the king and the promises of the protecting goddesses. The design symbolizes the transformation of the king into the new-born sun carried on the wings of the sky-god Horus. The pectoral was designed to hang from straps of four strings.

99, 100 Details of a pectoral, complete with its straps and counterpoise, found in a box in the tomb of Tut-ankh-amun (see Plate 156). Pectoral (Plate 99) and counterpoise (Plate 100), gold of rather poor quality, silver, translucent quartz and calcite set in coloured cements, green, red, black, light blue and dark blue glass: electrum and dark blue glass beads. Pectoral, H. 11·5 cm., W. 14·1 cm; counterpoise, H. 8·4 cm., W. 7·8 cm.; straps, L. 34·3 cm. Carter Cat. No. 269, I, J, Q.

The pectoral is in the form of a kiosk with the base decorated with eight groups of *heh*-signs signifying 'eternity'; and a starry firmament beneath the architrave. Within this naos the king in the Blue Crown, imbricated cloak and feathered garb of his coronation, and holding his sceptres stands before the deities of Memphis seated on thrones. On the left is the lion-headed Sekhmet who holds out a notched palm-rib symbolizing long years of rule; and on the right, Ptah who gives life and power from the sceptre he holds in both hands. Behind Sekhmet is the king's *Ka*, with another of his names surmounted by a crowned falcon. Behind Ptah is a kneeling figurine of Eternity holding notched palm-ribs and supporting a uraeus wearing the solar disk and coiled upon a *neb*-sign. Inscriptions declare that Sekhmet promises the king 'years of eternity'; and Ptah, 'Life, Power and Well-being.'

The counterpoise is also of kiosk shape but the columns are of clustered papyrus-bud form and the base has a bar from which hang fourteen beaded tassels, eight of which end in little gold fishes. Within the kiosk, the king wears the Blue Crown and, holding a sceptre, sits on a throne before the winged goddess Maet, from whom he receives the sign of life.

Each strap is made of fifteen plaques of four different designs, the names of the king alternating with his titles and with good wishes, and each is bordered with strings of beads.

There is little doubt from the design of this jewel which shows the king as a terrestrial ruler, and its location within the tomb, that it was not part of his funerary equipment but had been made for his coronation.

101 Pectoral, with necklace and counterpoise, of gold, electrum, lapis lazuli,

green felspar, calcite (some inlays set with coloured cements), white, green, light blue and dark blue glass. Pectoral, H. 11·8 cm., W. 10·8 cm.; counterpoise H. 6·2 cm. (without tassels), W. 6·8 cm. Carter Cat. No. 269, K, from the same box as Plate 99 (see Plate 156).

The pectoral ornament shows a golden bark carrying the electrum crescent and disk of the moon over the waters of the firmament, symbolized by the lotus buds and flowers springing from the *pet*-sign for heaven, resting upon alternate light and dark blue supports. The straps consist of four strings of lapis lazuli, gold, carnelian, and black resin barrel-beads alternating with lapis lazuli, felspar, and gold ball-beads. Groups of the last are soldered together to form spacer-bars. The counterpoise is in the form of a lotus flower, flanked by buds and two rosettes, furnished with a bar from which hang nineteen beaded tassels. The clasp fastens on its right-hand side by means of a retractable pin. A tasselled cord is attached to the lunar crescent for anchoring the pectoral in position when it is being worn. This is another example of a jewel worn by the king during his lifetime.

102 Pendant, of gold, electrum, lapis lazuli, carnelian, red and blue glass. H. 14·1 cm., W. 16·4 cm. Carter Cat. No. 267, I. Found in a casket (see Plate 153).

The ornament is in the form of a sated vulture made in gold cloisonné-work inlaid with glass and stones. The body is only slightly curved and the tail outspread; the talons hold *shen*-signs. The head and neck of the bird, however, are worked in the round, apparently by casting. The head is surmounted by an electrum *Atefu*-crown with inlaid feathers, probably indicating that it is the goddess Nekhebet of Upper Egypt who is represented here. The back is chased and fitted with rings to take the suspension cord which ends in tassels.

103 Pectoral, gold, lapis lazuli, blue, red and green glass. H. 6·5 cm., W. 11 cm. Carter Cat. No. 256, PPP. Found on the mummy of Tut-ankh-amun.

The bird is the sociable vulture, representing Nekhebet, the patron goddess of Upper Egypt. The body is worked in the round, the head being cast separately. The back is of plain gold with the details chased; a pectoral in the form of the king's cartouche hangs from straps around the neck of the bird. The wings are displayed, the talons gripping *shen*-signs. The suspensory straps consist of alternate plaques of gold and lapis lazuli threaded on four strings, two of which take the outer border of gold and blue glass beads. The clasp (not shown) is in the form of a pair of resting falcons of cloisonné-work.

This jewel is important as being one of the earliest examples of enamelling. The cloisons of the body, tail and the greater coverts of the wings are filled with lapis lazuli-coloured glass, apparently introduced in powdered form and fired *in situ*. The lesser coverts are filled with red glass and a crater formed by an air bubble may be seen in nearly every cell (see p. 128).

104   *Above:* Pendant, gold, inlaid with carnelian, turquoise, green felspar, lapis lazuli and calcite. H. 9 cm., W. 10·5 cm. Carter Cat. No. 267, A. Found with Plate 102 (see Plate 153).

A scarab of lapis lazuli, with falcon wings in cloisonné-work, supports between his forelegs the red disk of the new-born sun as he stands upon a *neb*-basket with three carnelian inlaid strokes, thus forming the prenomen of the king, Neb-kheperu-re ('Master of Transformations like Re'), besides representing the birth of the sun-god. The back of the jewel is of plain gold with chased details. A horizontal tube behind the disk was for suspension on a chain or cord. This is doubtless another of the king's secular jewels returned to the wrong box.

Below: Pendant, gold, inlaid with lapis lazuli, carnelian, turquoise, and light blue glass: the eye of obsidian, or black glass. H. 11·7 cm., W. 12·6 cm. Carter Cat. No. 267, M1. Found with Plate 102 (see Plate 153).

The jewel is in the form of a falcon with wings outspread, bearing on its vertex the red disk of the rising sun, and holding *shen*-signs in its talons which are also attached to the wings by *ankh*-signs, one being damaged. The back is of plain gold with the details chased and has four rings attached for the suspensory cord which ends in tassels. This jewel, representing the king as the newly risen Horus, is of traditional form, a similar falcon but on a much smaller scale and with most of its inlays missing, having been found among the Dahshur treasures (*cf.* Plate 44). It is probably part of the king's coronation regalia re-packed into the wrong box.

105   *Outer:* A scarf or stole, probably part of a sacerdotal dress. L. 69·5 cm., W. 4·6 cm. Carter Cat. No. 269, O. Found with Plate 99 (see Plate 156).

The ornament is made of seven strings of blue faience disk beads, caught at intervals by thirteen spacer bars made of graduated tubes of gold soldered together so that it assumes a horse-shoe shape. The terminals are in the form of gold cartouches chased with the names of the king, and with epithets declaring him to be beloved of Sokar and Ptah of Memphis. At the lower edge of each terminal is a row of four *ankh*-signs (one broken). This object, more of a garment than a jewel, was probably worn around the neck of the king, in the reverse position to that shown on the plate, like a stole when officiating in his capacity of chief priest of the Memphite cults.

Inner: Pendant, gold, inlaid with lapis lazuli (blue glass?), carnelian and obsidian (for eyes). H. 7·4 cm., W. 11·7 cm. Carter Cat. No. 267, O. Found with Plate 102 (see Plate 153).

Similar in design and construction to Plate 103, except that the head of the bird is in a different position and the back is quite plain. Two rings are affixed to take the tasselled suspensory cord, remains of which existed at the time of discovery, but which here has been restored, as is also the case with Plates 102 and 104.

106 Pectoral, gold, silver, calcedony, carnelian, calcite set in coloured cements, lapis lazuli, turquoise, obsidian, green, red, blue, black and white glass. H. 14·9 cm., W. 14·5 cm. Carter Cat. No. 267, D. Found with Plate 102 (see Plate 153).

The lower part of this complicated jewel consists of a floral garland originating from the lotus flower pendants often seen in Old Kingdom representations. It is here greatly elaborated to become three such flowers alternating with two buds and two outer blooms of cornflower shape, separated from each other by six roundels representing stylized marguerites. The central parts show a solar falcon in cloisonné-work, its wings outspread and its talons holding *shen*-signs and the heraldic flowers of Lower and Upper Egypt—the lotus flower and the flowering rush. The head and body of the bird have been replaced by a chalcedony scarab, worked in the round, representing Khepri the sun-god at dawn. Flanking Khepri are protective solar uraei. Instead of the usual disk of the sun, the forelegs of Khepri support an elaborate symbol representing both the sun and the moon. It takes the form of a celestial bark bearing the left eye of the sky-god Horus which was miraculously restored by Thoth, the ibis-headed god of the moon, after it had been torn to pieces in the contest between Horus and the storm-god Seth. This is flanked by protective solar uraei upholding the crescent and disk of the moon. Within this symbol is a figure of the king supported by the ibis-headed Thoth and the falcon-headed sun-god Re, the two former wearing the crescent and disk of the moon, the last the solar disk.

This jewel is an elaborate rebus on the prenomen of the king, the sun disk being replaced by the celestial bark and its crew, the *neb*-sign evidently being attached to the calyx of each lotus flower, and the three plural strokes becoming the thirteen roundels below the scarab. But it also symbolizes the birth of the sun and the moon, and was doubtless part of the king's coronation regalia when a new son of the sun-god was born to rule Egypt at the beginning of the old lunar year.

107 *Left:* Clasp, gold, inlaid with lapis lazuli, carnelian and green felspar. H. 5·6 cm., W. 5·6 cm. Carter Cat. No. 261, L. Found with Plate 98 (see Plate 154). This fastening is probably an element in a bracelet or belt, the design of which is based upon the king's name. The scarab supports a *neb*-basket with its rear legs, and flanking the sun-disk held between its front legs are two *h*-signs, making the group for 'eternity'. On each side of this element is hinged a uraeus surmounted by a sun-disk, and penetrating a *shen*-sign. A removable pin allows the clasp to be opened. The right side is perforated by twenty-eight holes; the left, with only seven, suggesting that this is the right-hand unit of a pair of such elements. When found, there were the remains of carnelian, turquoise, lapis lazuli and gold bead borders. The rest had been stolen in antiquity.

Centre: Pendant, gold inlaid with lapis lazuli, green felspar and calcite set in coloured cement. H. 7·5 cm., W. 8·2 cm. Carter Cat. No. 267, P. Found with Plate 102 (see Plate 153).

The design of this jewel is also based upon the elements in the king's prenomen Neb-khepheru-re (*cf.* Plate 104). The scarab is carved from pieces of lapis lazuli set in gold cloisons. The falcon wings in chased gold are more stylized in order to fit into a circular shape. A horizontal tube soldered to the rear took a suspensory chain or cord, now missing.

Right: Clasp, or counterpoise, gold and silver, inlaid with lapis lazuli, calcite set with coloured cements, green, red, and blue glass. H. 6·8 cm., W. 6 cm. Carter Cat. No. 267, B. Found with Plate 102 (see Plate 153).

The central element is a cartouche containing the king's prenomen surmounted by the crescent moon and disk, the latter of silver heavily tarnished. This is supported on each side by a uraeus bearing the solar disk. The lower bar is perforated with nine holes evidently to take bead tassels now missing (*cf.* Plate 100). The right-hand uraeus slides on a tongue within a groove to form a fastening. Suspensions behind the solar disks are each perforated to take six strings of beads or plaquettes now lost.

108   Counterpoise, gold of inferior quality, lapis lazuli, calcite, obsidian, green, light blue and dark blue glass. H. 6·9 cm., W. 8·2 cm. Carter Cat. No. 267, E. Found with Plate 102 (see Plate 153).

The design shows the figure of Eternity, flanked by uraei, kneeling on a mat to uphold the protective eye of Horus (*q.v.* Plate 106), with the *Tyet* girdle of Isis in place of the usual tadpole-and-*shen*-sign. This, however, is seen at the base of each notched palm-rib, signifying, 'myriads of years of rule', which forms the outer border of the jewel and supports the heavens forming its top. At either end of this is a terminal bar; the sliding portion of one, forming a clasp, is missing. The other is pierced to take a strap of six strings. The lower bar is hinged and perforated to take eighteen beaded tassels, some ending in fishes of red and yellow gold (*cf.* Plate 100), but of these only a few remain and are not shown here.

109   *Above*: Bracelet, gold, amethyst, lapis lazuli, carnelian and red jasper. L. of wrist-band, 13·5 cm., W. 1·9 cm.; H. of centre piece 4·1 cm., L. 4·5 cm. Carter Cat. No. 269, M. Found with Plate 99 (see Plate 156).

The centre piece is formed of an amethyst scarab bearing the king's prenomen set in an open oval gold plaque decorated with gold granules (*cf.* Plate 129). It is flanked by inlaid solar uraei, and bordered by ring beads of stone and gold. The underside is inscribed on the border surrounding the base of the scarab with the titles and prenomen of the king 'Living Forever'. The wrist-band consists of four strings of beads threaded between eight gold spacers. The beads are in the form of scarabs, *wedjet*-eyes, and spheroids. The open-work gold scarabs are inscribed with the prenomen of the king.

Below: Bracelet, gold, lapis lazuli, carnelian, light blue and dark blue glass, calcite. L. of wrist-band 10·7 cm., W. 3·5 cm. H. of centre piece 6·6 cm., W. 5·1 cm. Carter Cat. No. 269, G. Found with Plate 99 (see Plate 156). The design of the centre piece is based upon the king's prenomen, the scarab being greatly enlarged and formed with gold cloisons inlaid with lapis lazuli and one piece of green glass. The sun-disk between its forelegs has been replaced by a cartouche bearing the king's prenomen (here placed upside down). Its rear legs hold the *neb*-basket inlaid with blue glass. The bracelet is composed of gold, blue glass, lapis lazuli, calcite, and electrum barrel beads, strung with carnelian, blue glass, and granular gold ring beads (*cf.* Plate 86 top) between eight gold spacers and upper and lower borders of gold ring beads. The fastening slides into a tongue on the right side of the scarab.

110 Bracelet, gold, lapis lazuli, turquoise, carnelian and quartz set in coloured cement. Internal diameters, max. 5·4 cm., min. 4·2 cm. Carter Cat. No. 269, N. Found with Plate 99 (see Plate 156).
   The bracelet consists of a massive, curved oval gold plate carrying the main design, hinged to a curved rectangular gold plate worked with a geometrical pattern and forming the connecting strap (*cf.* Plate 129). A retractable pin at one of the hinges serves as a fastener. The main design is a scarab, the body of which is formed of gold cells set with pieces of lapis lazuli; its legs are of gold. The oval plate on which it is mounted is decorated with strings of gold granules and a gold, carnelian, turquoise and lapis lazuli block border. The two trapezoidal spacers are filled with a floral design of a mandrake fruit flanked by two poppy buds and marguerites.
   All these scarab bracelets, Plates 109, 110, appear to be part of the king's personal jewels worn in his lifetime.

111 Vulture collar and counterpoise, gold inlaid with coloured glass. H. 36·5 cm., W. 46·4 cm. Found on the mummy of King Tut-ankh-amun. Late XVIIIth Dynasty. In the Cairo Museum. Carter Cat. No. 256MMM.
   This collar of 'Nekhebet' or of 'the Vulture' (*cf.* Plate 72) is flexible being composed of 250 separate elements threaded together by means of rings on strings that originally were packed with gold ring beads to form external and internal lines of gold in the design. Each element is fitted with cloisons and inlaid with coloured glass. The body and tail of the bird and the lesser coverts of the wings are inlaid with bright turquoise blue and red and dark blue glass, whereas towards the tips of the primaries and secondaries, gold becomes dominant. The reverse is chased with the same pattern of feathering and each element is numbered according to the part of the wing to which it belongs. This jewel gives an indication of the design and appearance of the vulture head-dresses of principal queens (*cf.* Plate 127), no actual example of which has survived. The *menkhet* counterpoise is also in cloisonné-

work and attached to the collar by gold wires. It follows the design of the pendant that hangs from the neck of the goddess Bat (*cf.* Plate 26).

112 Bracelets of King Tut-ankh-amun, gold, electrum, carnelian, green felspar, turquoise, lapis lazuli and coloured glass. Average diam. 5·4 cm. Late XVIIIth Dynasty. In the Cairo Museum. Carter Cat. Nos. (from top to bottom and left to right) 256X, OO-SS, SS(bis); AAA, ZZ, YY, XX, WW, DDD.

The two sets of bracelets here illustrated were found on the left and right arms respectively of the mummy of Tut-ankh-amun. They fall into two broad groups—those of rigid half-cylinder design with hinge-pin fastenings (*viz.* X, PP, RR, ZZ and WW) and the remainder (with the exception of XX) which are in the form of flexible bead bracelets. Those of the first type resemble closely in their construction the specimen illustrated in Plate 110 and the later bracelets of Ramesses II (see Plate 129), having a curved oval front-plate and a curved rectangular rear strap of several gold tubes. Bracelets RR and WW are particularly close to the Ramessid specimens, having plaques of hardstone (brown jasper (?) and turquoise) in gold settings embellished with granular work. Of the other bracelets in this group two (PP and ZZ) have designs based upon the *wedjet*-eye and form a pair. The remaining specimen (X) has the design of the crowned Nekhebet vulture inlaid in carnelian and other details in hardstones and glass.

The flexible bracelets follow the pattern of those illustrated in Plate 109, having straps of faience, glass and gold beads kept in position by gold bead spacers. The main design in this group is the scarab (QQ, SS, YY) and the *wedjet*-eye (OO, AAA) in a pale green stone, lapis lazuli and carnelian. The two lowermost bracelets in each column also form a pair and have disks of lapis lazuli in gold settings decorated with granular-work.

The plain bead bracelet (XX) represents a compromise between these two types. The front half-cylinder is semi-flexible consisting of carnelian, amethyst, green felspar and gold ball beads between ring beads of gold all threaded on gold wires. The rear cylinder is of gold decorated in granular work and inlaid with carnelian and blue and green glass.

All these bracelets appear to have been worn by the king in his lifetime.

113 Floral Broad Collar. D. 47 cm. Found in a cache in the Valley of the Kings, Western Thebes in 1908 by T. M. Davis. Late XVIIIth Dynasty. In the Metropolitan Museum of Art, New York. Reg. No. 09.184.216.

Three such collars, two semi-circular in shape, were found almost intact with other material which is believed to be the debris left over from a funerary banquet held on the occasion of the burial of King Tut-ankh-amun. They were apparently worn by guests at the function and afterwards ceremonially buried. The one illustrated is composed of olive leaves, cornflowers, and the berries of the woody nightshade interspersed with bright blue faience disks strung on strips of palm leaf and sewn to a backing of papyrus which is bound at the edges with red cloth. Cords are sewn to the ends of the inner edge to act as ties. Such collars are the natural archetypes for more permanent versions in faience or cloisonné-work (cf. Plates 71, 125, 146).

114 *Menyet*, bronze, faience, stone and glass. L. (of counterpoise) 14·5 cm. Excavated in the ruins of the palace of Amenophis III at Western Thebes in 1911 by the Metropolitan Museum Egyptian Expedition. In the Metropolitan Museum, New York, Reg. No. 11.215.450.
The *menyet* is a ceremonial object particularly associated with the goddess Hathor whose priestesses are commonly shown holding the emblem. Queens and great ladies when officiating as priestesses also wore or carried it (cf. Plate 116). On rare occasions it was worn or carried by men (cf. Plate 151), particularly by priests of Hathor, and it is also worn by the god Khons. Originally it consisted of a necklace of small beads on numerous strands the ends of which are caught into two strings of heavier beads, each ending in a counter-weight. Statues of the earlier periods sometimes show these two counterpoises hanging down the back of the wearer (cf. Fig. 11); but, by the beginning of the New Kingdom, they had been fused into one such weight, though in votive faience *menyets* a thin groove is frequently incised around the outside edges, as though two counterpoises had been stuck together one on top of the other. A recent ingenious attempt to see in the *menyet* counterpoise a development of the 'paddle doll' of the early Middle Kingdom seems rather wide of the mark. The *menyet* here illustrated is a rare example of an actual specimen, not an *ex voto* and shows a single heavy bronze counterpoise to which is attached two strings of stone, polychrome glass and faience beads connecting with the ends of the necklace proper. This consists of multiple strings of small blue faience ring beads capped at each end with a shallow bronze cone.

115 *Menyet* counterpoise, bronze. H. 17·2 cm. Later XVIII Dynasty. In the Metropolitan Museum, New York, Reg. No. 51.57.2.
This counterpoise takes an openwork form which is not uncommon in the reign of Amenophis III and seems to represent Hathor with the features of Queen Tiye. It is surmounted by the head of the goddess wearing a diadem with uraeus and her characteristic horns and disk. In the openwork design below, she appears in her human aspect as an elegant queen holding a papyrus sceptre, and also in her animal guise as a wild cow in a papyrus skiff in the waters of the papyrus marshes.

116 Painting in the chapel of tomb No. 96 of the Mayor of Thebes, Sen-nufer, at Western Thebes. Reign of Amenophis II, Middle XVIIIth Dynasty.
Sen-nufer, and his wife Meryt, are being lustrated by the ritual priest who

pours streams of purifying water over them. Sen-nufer wears gala costume and holds a staff of office in one hand and a formal bouquet in the other. His jewellery is elaborate. He wears large gold-ear-rings, double armlets on each arm and bracelets at the wrist, the one on his right forearm resembling that shown on Plate 58. Around his neck is a gold *shebyu*-collar worn over a Broad Collar of blue and green beads. A gold and silver pectoral in the form of two heart-symbols hangs on his breast. In addition to the fillet tied around her brows, Meryt, holding a lotus flower, wears large gold ear-rings and bracelets and armlets to match her Broad Collar (*cf.* Plate 64). In her right hand she carries a *menyet* amulet of gold and red and blue beads (*cf.* Plate 114); and in her left, a formal bouquet and a golden sistrum, the latter for use in her capacity as a 'Singer of Amun'.

117   X-ray photograph of the mummy of the architect Kha in the Turin Museum. Reign of Amenophis III. Later XVIIIth Dynasty.

In 1966 the mummies of Kha and his wife Meryt, which have not been unwrapped since the finding of their intact burial at Deir el-Medina by an Italian expedition in 1906, were X-rayed and were found to be wearing jewellery (*cf.* Plates 20–22). The illustration shows the upper part of the body of Kha with the following ornaments visible. On his forehead, a *werweret* amulet carved in the form of a snake's head, probably of carnelian or red jasper. In the region of his left and right ears are metal ear-rings probably of disk type with stirrups similar to those of Tut-ankh-amun but less elaborate (*cf.* Plates 121, 122). Around his neck is a single *shebyu*-necklace of heavy metal beads, probably in gold (*cf.* Plate 116), and he has a *tyet* (girdle-tie) amulet, probably in red jasper. Also to be seen are two lengths of a metal chain from which hangs a large heart scarab around his neck. Unlike Wah (*cf.* Plates 20–22), Kha and Meryt have not yet been unwrapped and their jewellery has not been brought to light.

118   Drawing by Robert Hay of Linplum made *c.* 1833 of a relief on the east wall of the tomb-chapel of Ay at Amarna. Late XVIIIth Dynasty. British Museum, Add. Ms. Nos. 29812–60.

The scene shows the award of gifts by Akhenaten, Nefert-iti and three of their daughters to the Master of the Horse, Ay, and his wife Tey, as they stand before the Palace Window of Appearances. The high dignitaries of the Court look on in admiring aclaim while Ay's servants caper about in delight and excitement. Grooms by their chariots await the return of the fortunate pair. Among the gifts that Ay and Tey are receiving are several *shebyu*-collars, signet-rings and vessels of gold, and textile gloves and fillets. In the upper right hand corner the palace guard sends a boy to find what all the commotion is about and receives the reply that Ay and Tey are being made 'persons of gold.' This drawing was made by Hay when he first opened the tomb of Ay and before it was damaged by subsequent vandals.

119 Relief on the western half of the 'Wall of the Annals' flanking the sanctuary of the temple of Amun at Karnak. Reign of Tuthmosis III. Middle XVIIIth Dynasty.

The sandstone blocks forming this wall are carved in bas-relief with a figure of Tuthmosis III presenting gifts to the temple of Amun. The portion here illustrated shows part of the inventory of jewels and metal vessels which were included in the sacerdotal furnishing. To the right of the summits of the two obelisks can be seen a bracelet of the type illustrated in Plate 58 and three others of the kind shown in Plate 64 (other examples will be found in the register immediately below). Also included are several necklaces and collars (*cf*. Plate 120) and the number of each type is also recorded on the relief.

120 Relief, portion, of limestone carved *en creux* from the tomb of Har-em-hab at Saqqara. L. 60 cm. Reign of Tut-ankh-amun. Later XVIIIth Dynasty. In the Rijksmuseum, Leyden.

The scene shows the General Har-em-hab being decorated before his king in the same manner as Ay in Plate 118. He stands before the royal kiosk with his arms raised in the gesture of jubilation while chamberlains load him with gold *shebyu*-collars of honour. Around his brows is a fillet tied with tapes at the back. On the crown of his hair has been placed a tall festal ointment cone. A second one, garnished with a garland, is held in a bowl by another functionary. The uraeus on Har-em-hab's brow is a later addition carved into the relief when he had attained the throne. The collars have fastenings furnished with pendants (*cf*, Plate 139) and are placed upon (basket-work) trays and protected by cloths.

121 *Left and right:* A pair of ear-rings, gold (tarnished in places), carnelian, calcite and quartz set in coloured cements, dark blue and green glass. H. 11·8 cm., W. 5·4 cm. Carter Cat. No. 269, A3. Found with Plate 99 (see Plate 156).

The fasteners consist of two ribbed tubes, one sliding in the other, capped with studs formed with two uraei (*cf*. Plate 122). To each of these, attached by stirrups hidden behind a spread-falcon, is a large, gold, flanged ring, the interior filled with a carved carnelian figurine of the king holding a sceptre and flanked on either side by a solar-uraeus, all upon a *heb*-festival sign. The periphery of the ring is threaded with a border of lenticular beads from which hang seven beaded tassels ending in gold and glass drop-beads.

Centre: A pair of ear-studs, gold inlaid with carnelian, light blue and dark blue glass, calcite set in coloured cement. H. 7·0 cm. Carter Cat. No. 269, A5. Found with Plate 99 (see Plate 156).

These studs penetrate the hole in the lobe of the ear and are closed with a cap, similar to the devices shown in the more elaborate examples. The outer boss is formed of a gold plate set with a carnelian dome and inlaid with glass and carnelian in a floral motif (*cf.* Plate 68, *top*). From the lower edge depend two solar uraei.

122 *Left and right:* A pair of ear-studs, gold inlaid with segments of glass. Diam. 2·5 cm. Carter Cat. No. 269, A6. Found with Plate 99 (see Plate 156).
These studs are smaller than the other examples in this group, the tubes being about 0·5 cm. in diameter suggesting that they were worn by the king in infancy before the holes in his ear-lobes had been distended to 0·75 cm. or more as measured on his mummy. The design incorporates two uraei as protective devices.
Centre: A pair of ear-rings, 'purple' gold, dark blue glass, black resin. H. 10 cm., W. 5·5 cm. Carter Cat. No. 269, A5. Found with Plate 99 (see Plate 156).
The construction is similar to that of Plate 121 (*left* and *right*). The tubes of the fasteners are capped at the outer ends with gold flowers. The stirrips connect these to hoops formed of dark resin beads, alternating with hollow gold ball-beads, formed into a hoop with blue glass rings between them. All the goldwork is coloured red (see p. 32) except for the applied yellow gold granules and wires. From the lowermost gold bead is hinged a bar from which hang seven beaded tassels ending in gold drops or flower finials.
All these ear-rings are undoubtedly examples of jewels worn by the king in his early years and put away as custom required when he reached the age of manhood. Although commoners are sometimes shown wearing ear-rings (see Plate 116) the Pharaoh never is, to the writer's knowledge.

123 The diadem, gold, inlaid with carnelian, chalcedony, turquoise, obsidian, light blue and dark blue glass. Average diam. 19 cm., W. of band 2 cm. Carter Cat. No. 256, 4O. Found on the mummy of Tut-ankh-amun.
This royal fillet is in the form of a 'boatman's-circlet' (see p. 130). To the band are attached the vulture head of Nekhebet in cast gold with obsidian eyes, and the cobra of Edjo, the tail of the latter winding into an arch to prevent the band from slipping over the brow. These symbols of the heraldic goddesses of Upper and Lower Egypt are detachable, sliding on T-shaped tongues into appropriate channels (*cf.* Plate 39). The band is decorated with carnelian roundels (some restored), rivetted into position by gold studs, on a ground of light and dark blue glass. The bow-knot at the rear consists of a roundel inlaid with chalcedony and flanked by a pair of papyrus umbels inlaid with turquoise (*cf.* Plate 83). From it hangs a pair of streamers; and another pair of side streamers hangs from the vicinity of the knot, each furnished with a protective uraeus (*cf.* Plate 150). All are inlaid in blue glass cloisonné-work and furnished with carnelian roundels to match the design of the fillet.

124 A statuette of King Amenophis III, gold cast solid, with glass bead necklace.

H. 5·0 cm. Carter Cat. No. 320, C. Found sealed in a nest of miniature coffins in the tomb of Tut-ankh-amun.

Amenophis III, wearing the Blue Crown and carrying sceptres, squats in the pose of the newly born sun-god and the newly arisen king (*cf.* Plate 128). The statuette was suspended from a loop-in-loop chain (see p. 87) and evidently worn as a personal jewel by the owner in honour of his father or grandfather. Pendants in the form of statuettes of gods, with perforated lugs by which they could be hung round the neck of the wearer, are known particularly from the later periods, in faience or metal (*cf.* Plates 128, 141 and 147). This specimen seems to be an early example of such an amulet, since Amenophis III was worshipped as a god even in his own lifetime.

125 Floral collar, polychrome faience, late XVIIIth Dynasty. D. 31·5 cm. In the Metropolitan Museum, New York, Reg. No. 40.2.5.

This example of costume jewellery is typical of the opulent and florid Amarna Period when the manufacture of faience and glass reached a peak of technical and artistic brilliance. The collar is an imitation in more permanent material of the festal collars made of ephemeral papyrus, flowers and leaves (*cf.* Plates 113). They were cheaper to produce than the expensive versions in gold and inlays (*cf.* Plates 66, 71) and could be supplied as favours to guests at banquets. Several faience collars of this type were found in the tomb of Tut-ankh-amun. The various beads were mass produced in clay moulds impressed with the shapes of cornflowers, mandrake fruits, dates, lotus petals, poppy petals, willow leaves and other natural forms. The colours of the originals were also imitated in the yellow, red-brown, blue, green, white and lilac glazes that the Egyptian had learnt to produce in faience. Each element in the five rows of beads in this collar—cornflowers, dates and lotus petals—is made with a ring bead at both extremities for threading on strings of similar ring beads to keep them in position. The large white faience terminals are inlaid with flower motifs (a technique which the faience-maker had also mastered at this period) and have five cylindrical pendants imitating the tasselled ends of the stringing threads. The tie-strings are modern restorations.

126 Coffin-board of a Singer of Amun, wood covered with gesso painted and varnished. XXIst-XXIInd Dynasty from Thebes. In the British Museum, Reg. No. 22542.

The painted decoration on the upper part of this coffin-board of a priestess of Amun (*c.* 1000–900 BC) is an elaboration of the natural flower garlands which were placed on the persons of the deceased during the burial ceremonies. A lower fringe of lotus flowers is visible and above this are rows of lotus petals, mandrake fruits, cornflowers and poppy petals. Berries and coloured beads which were added to actual examples (*cf.* Plate 113) are here reduced to rows of chequers.

127 Queen Nefert-ari makes an offering to Osiris. Part of a wall painting in the tomb of the queen in the Valley of the Queens, Western Thebes. XIXth Dynasty, *c.* 1280 BC.

The detail shows the chief wife of Ramesses II during the earlier part of his reign offering water to the god of the dead before a piled-up altar. She wears the head-dress of a principal queen in the form of a vulture, no actual example of which has survived, but which must have been made of plain or inlaid gold elements threaded together to form a flexible covering (*cf.* Plates 62 and 111). This is surmounted by a squat modius carrying a sun-disk and two tall flickering feathers made of gold. In her ears she wears an ornament of silver, probably representing a papyrus umbel, its stalk passing through the hole in her ear-lobe. Around her neck is a Broad Collar probably made of inlaid plaques imitating flower petals, mandrake fruits and chevron borders (*cf.* Plates 71, 125). On her wrists are inlaid silver bracelets of traditional form (*cf.* Plate 64).

128 Pendant, gold and decayed glass (?) inlays. H. 7·2 cm. Probably XIXth Dynasty. In the Museum of Fine Arts, Boston, Reg. No. 68.836.

This pendant is made of gold and represents the king, probably Ramesses II, as the young sun-god at his birth from a lotus flower, which rises out of the primeval waters to open and reveal him within. The figure appears to have been made by hammering thick gold foil over a stone or wooden core and filling the two half shells with fine clay before soldering them along their seams (*cf.* Plate 78). The lotus flower is made in the cloisonné technique and soldered on separately. The collar, with its drop beads, has been inserted into an area sunk on the obverse after the figure was made. The same process appears to have been employed in forming the comma-shaped depression for the insertion of the side-lock, probably of lapis lazuli, now missing. The counterpoise to the collar has been made separately and soldered in place. The reverse is chased with the details that on the obverse are inlaid. The sun-disk is made separately and affixed by two rings set apart so that they engage with a central ring soldered near the crown of the figure. Through the three rings a stud passes which also engages rings on the ends of the ferrules that terminate the double loop-in-loop suspensory chain.

129 A pair of bracelets, gold and lapis lazuli. Greatest diam. 6·6 cm., greatest width 6 cm. From Tell Basta, XIXth Dynasty. In the Cairo Museum, Cat. Nos. 52575–6.

These bracelets were part of the Tell Basta Treasure (see p. 12), and are examples of the rigid type that makes its appearance at the beginning of the XVIIIth Dynasty (*cf.* Plate 54). They were presumably part of the temple vestments, probably decorating a wooden cult statue of Ramesses II. The main half-cylinder carries a dome-shaped piece of lapis lazuli forming the body of a goose with two heads and a common tail. The outline of this insertion determines the shape of the half-cylinder which is decorated with granules, plain, beaded and twisted wires soldered in position with great skill (*cf.* Plates 68, 109, 112) by the colloidal process (see p. 99). The other half is a plain gold band hinged to the major portion and decorated with parallel narrow half-tubes alternately plain and ribbed. Flanking one hinge on the front is a cartouche containing the prenomen of Ramesses II worked in repoussé; and on the other, a panel of lozenges in granular work.

130–131 Jewellery from the Theban tomb of an infant princess, gold. Late XIXth Dynasty. In the Cairo Museum.

In 1908, Edward Ayrton, excavating for Theodore M. Davis, discovered a small pit tomb (No. 56), in the Valley of the Kings at Western Thebes, mostly full of mud and debris which had been washed into it, presumably after it had been opened in antiquity by thieves who partly rifled it. Among the objects which were recovered from the dried mud were a number of jewels inscribed with the names of Queen Twosre and her first husband King Sethos II (*c.* 1210 BC). From this circumstance it has generally been assumed that the tomb was a cache of jewellery belonging to the queen; but its presence near a decayed miniature coffin and other clues rather point to its having been deposited in the tomb to supplement the possessions of an infant daughter of Twosre and Sethos II (see pp. 99–100).

130 *Centre:* Pair of ear-rings, gold. H. 13·5 cm. In the Cairo Museum, Cat. Nos. 52397–8.

The ear-rings are of a similar construction to those of Tut-ankh-amun shown in Plates 121 and 122, and since they are inscribed with the cartouches of Sethos II may have belonged to him when he first came to the throne as a minor, though it is perhaps more likely that they were specially made for this burial (see below). The basis of the design is a concave corolla fluted into eight petals with a hemispherical boss at its centre. Each alternate petal is inscribed with the names of Sethos II worked in repoussé. This flower-form is soldered to a striated tube into which fits another similar tube, its opposite end closed by an inscribed hemispherical boss balancing the weight of the flower. This fastening, which penetrates a large hole in the ear-lobe, forms the means of suspension for an elaborate pendant attached to it by two striated stirrups and consisting of two parts. The first is a trapezoid, also inscribed on both faces with the names of the king, and having rings attached to its lower edge for taking a bar from which hangs the second part. This takes the form of three large and four smaller flower shapes, probably meant to be stylized cornflowers or poppy seed-heads. They are each of fluted spherical form with a wide bell-shaped crown attached to a striated tubular stalk. The workmanship is somewhat careless and the finish summary, the soldering of the two hemispheres which form the mass of each pendant being readily visible. The total effect, however, is an ear ornament of bold, if barbaric, appearance.

Outer: A necklace, gold. H. (of pendants) 2·1 cm. D. (of beads) 0·7 cm. In the Cairo Museum, Cat. No. 52679.

A considerable number of loose elements which have been threaded into two necklaces, one in Cairo and the other in New York, were found by Davis and Ayrton in their clearance of pit tomb No. 56. Each of the two different elements are built up with great skill from a number of wire rings of three or four different diameters soldered together to give the outline of a sphere with conical appendage imitating a flower or seed-carpel, as in the ear-rings on the same plate. Like them also, the open-work carpels are soldered to a stalk made of a piece of striated sheet rolled into a tube and soldered with a loop at the distal end. This is the earliest example of a filigree technique which has persisted in certain metal jewellery to the present day, particularly in the Mediterranean area. In Egypt it was imitated also in the manufacture of certain open-work beads in faience, a material which often copied metal-work forms.

131 *Centre:* A pair of ear-rings, electrum, carnelian and blue faience. D. 4·6 cm. From a pit-tomb (No. 56) in the Valley of the Kings, Western Thebes. XIXth Dynasty. In the Cairo Museum, Cat. No. 52399.

The ear-rings were found scattered among the other mud-encased jewellery in the pit-tomb and have been re-assembled with a fair degree of probability. Each penannular ring, 1·4 cm. in diameter, is made by soldering half-shells of electrum hammered in a suitable mould and closing the ends with circular perforated plates. The outer seam is masked by a wire soldered along the periphery. To the lower arc of the ring have been soldered six small rings (one missing in the right-hand example) from which hang pendants in the form of blue faience flower calices set in electrum mounts which have apparently lost a large ball bead (*cf.* the shape of the pendants on the ear-rings in Plate 130). Other pendants are in the form of carnelian buds, also mounted in electrum, and ring beads in carnelian and faience.

Outer: Circlet, gold. D. 17·0 cm. From a pit-tomb (No. 56) in the Valley of the Kings, Western Thebes. XIXth Dynasty. In the Cairo Museum, Cat. No. 52644.

The coronet consists of a circle of thick gold sheet, 0·4 cm. in width, perforated at irregular intervals, varying from 2·5 to 4·3 cm. with sixteen holes for attaching the ornaments in the form of flowers. These have been made by burnishing gold foil into stone or wood moulds, and are similar in design to those on the ear-rings shown in Plate 130 except that they each have ten petals instead of eight. Five of these petals are inscribed alternately with the name of King Sethos II and Queen Twosre. In the centre of each flower is a button representing the pad of pistils to the back of which is soldered a looped shank allowing the flower to be attached to the band by a fastening which has not survived, but which has been replaced by iron wire. A notable feature of this coronet is that some at least of the flowers were made of coloured gold (see p. 32), though the central boss appears to have been of plain metal. It is difficult to reach any firm conclusion owing to the burying of the jewel in mud for many centuries and the subsequent cleaning it has undergone, but it seems possible that originally the flowers assembled on the band were alternately of red and yellow gold.

The adult jewellery found in this tomb has all the appearance of having been made somewhat carelessly from flimsy materials; but the various pieces are *en suite*, their design being based upon a floral motif, perhaps a poppy or anemone, 'the lilies of the field'. Despite the fact that they are inscribed with the names of Queen Twosre and her husband, Sethos II, it is doubtful whether they were made for her, since they do not bear the insignia of a reigning queen or an heiress princess. The assumption is, therefore, that they were made hurriedly for the equipment of the deceased infant, whose other jewels, as distinct from her funerary amulets, included a finger-ring of her ancestor Ramesses II.

132 Ramesses III and his son, Amen-(hir)-khopeshef being received by Ptah-Tanen. Part of a wall-painting in the tomb of the prince in the Valley of the Queens, Western Thebes. XXth Dynasty *c.* 1180 BC.

Ramesses III and his son are shown in full regalia, the prince acting as a fan-bearer. The king wears a necklace and Broad Collar, armlets and bracelets, and has a belt made of inlaid gold plaques from which hangs in front an apron from a leopard head, also made in cloisonné. At the rear of the belt is a bead-work tail (*cf.* Plate 9). The prince wears a Broad Collar and bracelets; his sash is woven with a pattern or has the design applied in needlework. The side-lock of infancy into which his hair is plaited is confined by an inlaid gold clasp which takes the form of a miniature bracelet.

133 Bracelets of the High Priest Pi-nudjem II, gold, carnelian and lapis lazuli. Outer diam. 6·8 cm. From Thebes, XXIst Dynasty. In the Cairo Museum, Cat. No. 52089.

These were found upon the mummy of the First Prophet (High Priest) of Amun, Pi-nudjem, who was the virtual ruler of Upper Egypt in the latter part of the XXIst Dynasty (*c.* 960 BC). They are variations upon the design of the rigid bracelet, the two half-cylinders being reduced to half-hoops, having their interior surfaces flattened to a ribbon. In cross-section each hoop is almost circular. They are joined at the hinge by a connecting wire on which is threaded a large lapis lazuli bead and, at the opposite pole, by a tongue which enters into a mortice and locks by means of a pin. Since the bead must have been in position when the wire connection was made, the method of fixing the latter must have been by cramping one end and not soldering both ends as has been maintained. Otherwise the lapis lazuli would have disintegrated under the excessive heat necessary, even if protected by a clay investment. The flat band which forms the basis of each bracelet has had transverse cloisons soldered to it to imitate a feather pattern; the compartments so formed have been filled with carnelian and lapis lazuli cut to shape and cemented in position. Near the clasp are two small rings which carry a number of tassels. Two of them consist of simple chains made from striated gold strip and have lapis lazuli pendants in the form of hexagonal pyramids. The others are made of lapis lazuli, carnelian and gold ring beads terminating in gold flowerettes, each having six conjoined petals.

134   Ear-plugs of Ramesses XI, gold. L. 16 cm., D. 5 cm. XXth Dynasty. In the Cairo Museum, Cat. Nos. 52323–4.

These massive gold ornaments were found by Mariette in 1859 on a decayed mummy buried in a sarcophagus beneath the sanctuary of the temple of Osiris at Abydos. They were evidently part of the jewellery of an unknown woman of the royal household. Each consists of a hollow, lenticular disk, grooved on the rim for inserting in the greatly enlarged holes in the ear-lobes which were fashionable among the ruling class at this period. On the outer face of this disk is soldered a plate decorated with a winged sun-disk in repoussé, and from which the pendants are suspended. The rest of the outer face carries five uraei worked in the round; three of them carry solar disks, while the outer pair wear *atefu*-crowns. Each is formed of two sheets of gold hammered to shape, the details are indicated in wires soldered in position. The reverse of the disk and the visible portion of the obverse are decorated with granules, twisted wires and plain wires (*cf.* Plates 112, 129) and carry the names of Ramesses XI, though they were not worn by him. The pendants take the form of solar uraei, each made of two plates soldered together, five in the first row attached to a bar and hinged to the disks. To the base-bar are attached seven loop-in-loop chains each fixed to the upper extremity of seven solar uraei which are free to move with the wearer. A feature of this jewel is that the disk is made of coloured ('purple') gold, the most recent ornament so far known to exhibit this technique (see p. 32).

135–140   Jewels from the royal tombs at Tanis, XXIst Dynasty. In the Cairo Museum. In 1939 Pierre Montet, excavating in the area of the main temple at Tanis, uncovered the substructures of a group of royal tombs which had been built in the precincts of King Psusennes I in the south-west corner of the site. The tombs of Psusennes I and Amenophthis of the XXIst Dynasty, and four kings of the XXIInd Dynasty were found, most of them reasonably intact though it was obvious that their burials had been disturbed and re-arranged in antiquity. From these deposits a number of jewels, nearly all destined for funerary use, were retrieved. Some of these later examples of the goldsmith's craft are of excellent workmanship and novel design, showing that the best standards achieved in the New Kingdom could be maintained on occassion in the Late Period, so far as can be judged from the little that has survived.

135 Bracelets of King Psusennes I, a pair, gold inlaid with lapis lazuli, carnelian and green felspar (?). H. 7 cm. Greatest diam. 8·0 cm. Montet Cat. Nos. 653–54.

These display a late variation on the design of the rigid bracelet consisting of two half-cylinders hinged at each end, one of the hinge-pins being retractable to form a clasp (*cf*. Plate 54). The bracelet is worked *à jour* in a cloisonné design. In each half-cylinder is a winged scarab (*cf*. Plates 93, 98) holding a sun-disk in his fore-legs and a *shen*-sign between his rear legs. This is flanked by the cartouches of the king bearing his two great names and surmounted by solar disks. Some of the inlays have been lost. These bracelets were found on the mummy of King Amenophthis.

136 *Upper*: Finger-rings, from the gold sheathed fingers of King Psusennes I, gold, lapis lazuli, red jasper and glazed steatite. Average D. 2·5 cm. Montet Cat. Nos. 566, 575, 570.

Each finger-ring is made of a penannular gold hoop with ends bent sharply to enter the rings on the fundae, and are held in position by a separate thin connecting wire threading the hole in the bezel and wrapped for some distance around the shank. Three of the rings are decorated with a *wedjet*-eye on the obverse and the name of the king on the reverse. The fourth has a simple scarab mounted in a massive gold funda. The rings appear to have been made for funerary use since for everyday wear the more robust rivetted design had long been in existence. The rings are photographed upside down in relation to the bracelet.

Lower: Bracelet one of a pair, gold and lapis lazuli. L. *c.* 19·5 cm. Montet Cat. No. 598.

From the position in which he found them, Montet argued that the pair of bracelets, of which one example is illustrated here, was worn just below the knee. Such knee ornaments, however, do not appear on the monuments at any period. A rigid bracelet or anklet was found in a similar anomalous position on the mummy of Tut-ankh-amun: the lengthy ritual of wrapping the royal corpse gave a number of chances for the embalmers to commit errors. Judging from the design of a rigid anklet belonging to Psusennes (see Plate 137 left) made *en suite*, this jewel is really a bracelet. It consists of two pairs of rectangular elements giving the names and titles of Psusennes in cartouches inlaid in cloisonné-work. Tubes are soldered to the edges of these elements, one to each short end and five to each long side, and are the gold bars in a striped border which, with lapis lazuli cylindrical beads, forms the upper and lower edges of the bracelet. Into the side-tubes hinge the lunate major elements, alternately in gold, and lapis lazuli set in gold.

This jewel exhibits a departure from the traditions of most Egyptian jewellery. The lunate motifs, however, can be seen already on the head-dress of a queen of Tuthmosis III (*cf.* Plate 62).

137   *Left:* Anklet, one of a pair, gold and lapis lazuli. H. 5 cm. Greatest diam. 6 cm. Montet Cat. No. 600.

These slightly tapering limb ornaments are one of the few incontrovertible examples of male anklets to have survived, having been found in position on the legs of King Psusennes I. The design is *en suite* with the bracelet shown in Plate 136 above, the greater half-cylinder being composed of similar lunettes alternately gold, and lapis lazuli set in gold. The upper and lower borders are also made of alternate tubes of gold and lapis lazuli. The lesser half-cylinder is hinged to the greater, one of the hinge-pins being retractable. This part is formed with a design of a winged scarab holding a sun-disk above a horizontal column-glyph, the whole comprising the king's prenomen flanked by two uraei, inlaid in lapis lazuli. Some of the inlays have fallen out and are missing.

Right: Bracelet, of King Psusennes I, one of a pair, gold. H. 4·3 cm. Outer diam. 6·1 cm., inner diam. 4·9 cm. Montet, Cat. No. 549.

This restrained but effective design of bracelet consists of two half-cylinders hinged together, one of the pins being retractable. Each half is composed of seven tubes of D-section, the outer surfaces being alternately smooth and ribbed. An inscription chased in the interior surface gives the titles and names of the king and his chief queen.

138   Collar, gold, of King Psusennes I. D. *c.* 20 cm. Montet Cat. No. 482.

This collar is a late version of five *shebyu* necklaces of honour fashioned into a single unit (*cf.* Plates 119, 120). The jewel is built up of 382 beads made by beating gold plate into a mould to form truncated cones 1·25 cm. in diameter, their bases perforated by large holes, and soldering each pair along their medial seams. Four groups of five such beads have been soldered into spacer bars which are distributed so as to divide the collar into five sectors. The fastener is a trapezoidal box 6·5 cm. long, the outer face of which has been worked in repoussé with a design imitating the reticulations of the separate strings of beads. The inner face is plain but chased with the titles and names of Psusennes I. The ends are formed as two lids perforated with five holes, to take the suspensory cords knotted at the rear, and furnished with a flange which is locked into the body of the fastener by two long retractable pins. Seven rings are soldered to the lower edge to take a bar holding the tasselled counterpoise, similar to that shown in Plate 139, but this has gone astray. This massive collar has been designed and made with a high degree of skill. It should, however, have been re-strung on a thicker pad of threads.

139   Collar, gold inlaid with 'Egyptian blue' (?), found on the mummy of King Amenophthis. D. 26 cm. L. (of pendant) 15 cm. Montet Cat. No. 644.

The collar consists of eleven strings of beads attached to an end piece in two parts. These fasten together by means of a pin traversing perforated lugs to form a trapezoidal element of gold inlaid on the face with chevrons of lapis lazuli (?), repeating the design that is formed in beadwork on the rest of the collar. These beads consist of perforated gold cylinders with dentated edges meshing into similar beads in imitation of lapis lazuli. Two groups of eleven gold beads have been soldered together each forming a spacer-bar which divides the collar into three sectors. At the lower edge of the outer half of the fastener are six rings to take a bar from which hang five tassels, each consisting of a string of beads presumed to be identical in design with those used for the collar, having a gold ferrule at the proximal end and a gold lotus bloom at the distal. From each lotus depends a pair of similar strings of beads ending in two other lotus flowers. Montet did not recover from the coffin of Amenophthis enough beads to complete the collar and tassel and he was inclined to believe that the missing beads had been lost by the wearer in life, and, for funerary purposes, they were replaced by cords. Montet's account is not sufficiently explicit to decide whether the collar was deposited on the mummy in a greatly delapidated state or some other explanation for the missing beads is possible. Sufficient evidence remains to show that the collar has been designed with great ingenuity and executed with considerable skill.

140 *Upper:* Pectoral of King Amenophthis, gold inlaid with lapis lazuli, much decayed. H. 9·8 cm., W. 10·6 cm. Montet Cat. No. 645.

The primeval shrine (*cf.* Plates 92–99) has a base, two pillars and an architrave all decorated with a block-border pattern and surmounted by a cavetto cornice carrying the winged disk of Horus of Edfu (*cf.* Plate 98). Within this, on a podium inscribed with the title and cartouche of Amenophthis, 'beloved of Osiris the Lord of Abydos', squats Isis, left, and Nephthys, right, supporting the scarab of Khepri who holds the new-born disk of the sun between his forelegs and the name of the king between his rear legs. Two pairs of rings on the upper edge of the cornice are the means of taking a suspensory chain similar to the example shown below. The design is feeble, the proportions and drawing of the two goddesses being particularly poor, and the execution careless. As this was essentially a funerary jewel few pains appear to have been taken to produce a masterpiece. The back is chased with the same design that appears in cloisonné on the front.

Lower: Pectoral of King Amenophthis, gold. H. 8·8 cm. W. 8·5 cm. Montet Cat. No. 646.

The pectoral is made of two sheets of gold, comprising the front and the back, soldered to an edging so as to form a thin hollow box, 2 mm. thick. The face is worked in repoussé and chasing with a scene showing, within the kiosk, left, the deceased King Amenophthis wearing the *nemes* head-cloth, broad collar, kilt and bull's tail, and offering incense to Osiris 'the Lord of Eternity', seated right. The inscription between them speaks of offering incense and libations 'three times' to 'his father Osiris'. At the base of the shrine is a dado of *djed* and *tyet* amulets. Above, the cavetto cornice is decorated with the winged disk of Horus of Edfu. A simple loop-in-loop chain, the ends soldered to ferrules, forms the means of suspension.

141 Pendant, gold, lapis lazuli, carnelian and frit. H. 9 cm. XXIInd Dynasty. In the Louvre, Paris. Reg. No. E.6204.
This technically superb jewel, here shown enlarged to over twice its proper size, is an elaborate example of a pendant representing a divinity (*cf*. Plate 124). A large ring soldered to the rear part of each figure provides the means of suspension. The three statuettes, cast in solid gold and affixed to a base-plate decorated with an inlaid block border, represent the Osirian trinity. In the centre is Osiris, with whom King Osorkon II is identified, squatting on a shrine, the body of which is carved from a block of lapis lazuli inscribed with the names of the king. He is protected on one side by his wife Isis, and on the other by his son, the falcon-headed Horus wearing the Double Crown. Isis is represented as an elegant woman wearing a tight-fitting dress and wearing a disk and cow-horns. Her long wig with lappets (*cf*. Plate 127) would have been fashioned of 'Egyptian blue' but this has decayed and entirely disappeared. The provenance of this piece, which was acquired by the Louvre in 1872, is unknown; but it has been suggested that it may have come from Tanis where the rifled tomb of Osorkon II was found by P. Montet in 1938. Certainly burials of the same period on this site had smaller but similar individual gold figurines of Isis, Horus and a squatting Osiris included in their funerary amulets.

142, 143 Pectoral, gold, inlaid with lapis lazuli, turquoise and steatite. W. 7 cm., H. 3 cm. Ptolemaic Period or later. From Saqqara. In the Brooklyn Museum, Reg. No. 37.804E.
Though this jewel was made in Hellenistic times, it is one of the best surviving examples of an amulet that is characteristically Egyptian in its design and technique. Such *ba*-bird pectorals are not uncommon in burials of the late period. They represent the *ba* or soul of the deceased as a human headed falcon with wings outspread, a concept which first makes its appearance in this form during the New Kingdom. An early example in cloisonné-work was found on the breast of the mummy of Tut-ankh-amun. The specimen illustrated here is much smaller and the cloisonné-work less elaborate but the body is made in the round, the human face bearing a particularly spiritualized expression. The front half of the body has apparently been made by forming a sheet of gold by the repoussé technique and soldering it to the base-plate comprising the wings. The lower half of the tail is formed of five inlays held in gold settings and are visible both on the obverse and

the reverse. Two ribbed loops were the means of attaching the jewel by sewing to the mummy wrappings.

144 Finger-ring, gold, traces of coloured glass inlay. D. 2·5 cm.

145 Pectoral, gold inlaid with coloured glass. H. 13 cm., W. 14 cm. Both excavated by A. Mariette in the Serapeum at Saqqara in 1850–4, XIXth Dynasty. In the Louvre, Paris, Reg. No. L. 75.

Most of the jewels which Mariette retrieved from the Serapeum and which are today in the Louvre were found in the funerary chapel of Kha-em-wese, the learned son of Ramesses II, who was also the High Priest of Ptah at Memphis and responsible in his day for conserving the monuments in the ancient necropolis at Saqqara and burying two of the sacred Apis bulls there. The objects illustrated in Plates 144, 145, came from this haul. The finger-ring is in a direct line of descent from the specimens of half a century earlier found in the tomb of Tut-ankh-amun (cf. Plate 91). It consists of a tripartite hoop with floral terminals. The central hoop has tubes soldered at intervals along its length but the glass cylinders that alternated with them have disappeared. The glass inlays are also missing from the bezel where the cloisons outlining the borders of poppy petals and lotus flowers may be clearly seen. The main decoration of the bezel is a span of chariot horses cast solid and soldered to their base-plate. They are shown cantering towards a somewhat problematic object which may have lost an essential part, but which appears to be a manger. The horses may represent any of the successive pairs that drew the royal chariots during the long reign of Ramesses II.

The pectoral is also in style and technique related to the Tut-ankh-amun specimens. The primeval shrine is formed of a trapezoidal frame of block-border pattern with a cavetto cornice fitted with anchorages at the ends to take the strings of the suspensory necklace. Within the kiosk a variation of the Collar of Edjo and Nekhebet (cf. Fig. 27) is to be seen in the vulture with outstretched wings combined with the cobra. Above this divine pair is a smaller winged deity in the form of a spread-falcon with the head of an animal, usually identified as a ram, supporting a cartouche containing the prenomen of Ramesses II. Two djed-colums in the lower corners fill in empty spaces and mechanically strengthen the jewel. The design and execution of the piece lack care and assurance. It is doubtful, for example, whether the head of the upper winged figure is that of a ram, it is more likely a bull's with horns depressed to fit in the space under the cartouche. In this pectoral, made for a quasi-royal burial, a decline in standards which is characteristic of the later reign of Ramesses II is quite evident.

146 Broad Collar, gold inlaid with carnelian, felspar, and lapis lazuli. W. 10·2 cm. Ptolemaic Period. In the Metropolitan Museum of Art, New York, Reg. No. 49.121.1.

This miniature inflexible collar is a rare example of a jewel made for a cult-statue. The design is traditional based upon the floral collar, but the complete flower heads shown as rosettes in the second row are characteristic of Late Period collars. The terminals are in the form of bars decorated with a block border pattern; and to these are hinged two lotus flower end-pieces connected by a loop-in-loop chain with a hook and ring fastening.

147 Statuette of a Nubian woman nursing apes. Blue and black faience. H. 14·6 cm. New Kingdom. In the Royal Scottish Museum, Edinburgh (ex Lee and Amhurst Collections), Reg. No. 1951.131.

The illustration is of an early example of a godling of popular origin who became more prominent in the Late Period, being transformed into the goddess Bast nursing kittens and the demi-god Bes, besides existing in a more stylized form in her own right as a Nubian with her hair dressed in characteristic bunches of curls. The importance of this statuette is that it is a unique representation of a person in Ancient Egypt wearing a nose-ring, the nose of the woman being pierced to take a silver ring which however, is missing (the tip of her nose has been broken off by the loss of the ring and is restored). The ape she is suckling wears a silver ring in the region of the ear or nose, and the animal at her feet also has a perforation to take a similar ornament. The woman has her ear-lobes pierced and an ancient silver ring is still in position in her right ear. The Egyptians, unlike the Hebrews (*Genesis* XXIV, 47; *Isaiah* III, 21) and the Cypriots (see note 24 on p. 144), did not wear nose-rings, though the body of a woman has been found at Abydos with a ring in her nose. She may, however, have been of foreign origin, perhaps a Nubian who, as this statuette shows, could wear on occasion a ring in the nose.

148 Copy by Nina de G. Davies of a painting from the south wall of tomb chapel No. 181 at Western Thebes. Later XVIIIth Dynasty.

This extract comes from the tomb of Neb-amun and Ipuky, two sculptors of Amenophis III who, as master craftsmen, were charged with the distribution of all kinds of valuable raw materials to the workshops in their charge. A workman under their supervision is weighing out gold for issue to his fellows for the various objects that are being manufactured. The arm of the balance see-saws on the knife-edge of the feather of Truth, and the head of the same goddess surmounts the upright. The weigher checks the indicator against the plumb-line. In the pans, a bull-head weight balances ten standard gold rings. To the left are some of the products of the workshop, a basket-work tray containing golden vessel and a Broad Collar of hardstone beads with inlaid lotus-flower terminals and counterpoise(*cf.* Plate 66), above (*i.e.* beside), a casket for jewels or other valuables (*cf.* Plates 152–3).

149 Lintel, limestone, portion of, carved in low relief from the tomb of Nefer-seshem-Psamtik at Memphis. L. 30 cm., H. 30 cm. XXXth Dynasty, fourth century BC. In the Cairo Museum, *J.E.* No. 10978.

This extract from a door lintel sculptured with a scene showing jewellery being brought to the tomb-owner, is concerned with the 'giving of collar(s)' as the inscription states, and is a notable piece of Ancient Egyptian antiquarianism since hardly any feature of the representation reflects the contemporary scene. The two women wear archaic costume with knotted shoulder-straps, a detail taken from men's costume in the Archaic Period. Their features, with emphasized lips and chins and two folds in the neck, are copied from Amarna models of a millennium earlier, as is the Nubian-type wig worn by the woman on the left. The latter holds a *menkhet* counterpoise and a Broad Collar by the tie-strings. Her companion clutches a similar collar and a necklace with a *sweret*-bead which must have been copied from a Middle Kingdom archetype (*cf.* Figs. 23, 24). Even the hieroglyph for 'collar' in the inscription is anachronistic, being a meticulous representation of a Broad Collar which was scarcely in current use. Nevertheless, if such ancient forms could be revived in this relief, there is warrant for believing that ancient fashions of jewellery could also have been copied by the contemporary craftsmen.

150 Statue fragment, black granite. H. 77 cm. XIXth Dynasty. From Tanis. In the Cairo Museum. Cat. No. 616.

This upper part of what was probably a seated statue of Ramesses II appears to be from the same studio as the famous statue of the Pharaoh in the Turin Museum and, like that, to have been made early in the reign as part of a coronation series. The king wears a fine-pleated robe and grasps the crook or *heka*-sceptre in his right hand; but in place of the Blue Crown of the Turin example he wears a short curled wig over his natural hair encircled by a diadem similar to that found on the mummy of Tut-ankh-amun (see Plate 123). The circlet, however, is decorated with a block-border pattern instead of roundels. It carries side streamers decorated at the ends with uraei wearing sun-disks, though the undulating bodies of the cobras are not emphasized. In addition, the king is shown wearing a Broad Collar of classic type with several rows of tubular beads and a lower border of drop-beads. On his right arm is a bracelet decorated with a *wedjet*-eye (*cf.* Plate 112).

151 Statue fragment, grey granite. H. 100 cm. XIIth Dynasty. From Mit Faris (Medinet el-Faiyum). In the Cairo Museum. Cat. No. 395.

This upper part of what was probably a striding statue of Ammenemes III is unique in showing the Pharaoh in sacerdotal attire. Apart from the peculiar heavy wig, he wears the leopard-skin cloak of a *setem*-priest, the head of the animal falling on the left shoulder and one fore-paw on the right. It is held together by a narrow bandolier passing over the chest and secured by a toggle. From the neck of the king depends a *menyet* amulet (*cf.* Plate 114) the many threads of its small beads hanging from two strings of large beads which end in two counterpoises, the tips of which are visible at the rear of the statue.

152 Jewel casket (reconstructed), ebony, redwood and ivory. Excavated in the tomb of Sit-Hathor-Yunet at Lahun in 1914. (see Plates 35–40). L. 35 cm., W. 24 cm., H. 25·5 cm. In the Metropolitan Museum of Art, New York, Reg. No. 16.1.2.

The reconstruction has been based upon the position of pieces of ivory inlay as they were found embedded in the mud of this tomb. The box had been adapted as a container for oil-jars, though it seems probable that originally it had been made with ivory-capped partitions for use as a jewel casket. The lid, as reconstructed, is decorated with three ivory panels giving three of the names of King Ammenemes III. A larger, and more elaborate jewel casket which has also been restored had a lid decorated with gold and hardstone inlays representing the goddess Bat (*cf.* Plate 46; Fig. 31). It was in containers of this kind that the Dahshur jewels were also stored (see Plates 27–31, 41, 42, 44–46).

153–156 Chests, gilded wood, ebony, ivory and faience. From the tomb of Tut-ankh-amun. XVIIIth Dynasty. In the Cairo Museum. Carter Cat. Nos. 261, 267, 269.

Most of the jewellery from the tomb of Tut-ankh-amun was found on the mummy of the king (*cf.* Plates 103, 111, 112, 123) and in boxes in the 'Innermost Treasury' shown in Plate 154. The finger-rings (Plate 91) and some faience collars (*cf.* Plate 125), came from an inlaid and gilded casket in the 'Antechamber'. Most of the pectorals (Plates 92–99) were stored in a gilded, pylon-shaped, chest surmounted by Anubis, the god of death, in the form of a black varnished, wood figure of a couchant dog with prick ears and a bushy tail (Plate 154). The interior of the chest was divided into compartments, in the largest of which were found eight pectoral jewels wrapped in linen and sealed. They had, however, been disturbed by the robbers who broke into the tomb soon after its closure. The depredations were not discovered until more than half the jewellery and goldwork had been stolen. The tomb was resealed by inspectors who cleared up in a hurried and perfunctory fashion, replacing objects haphazardly in the wrong boxes.

Other jewels were found in a box decorated with ebony and ivory marquetry (Plate 153) which was first in the row of such furniture flanking the Anubis pylon (see Plate 154). On its vaulted lid was an ink inscription reading 'golden ornaments [?] of the funerary procession made in the bier

[?] chamber of Neb-kheperu-re' (*i.e.* Tut-ankh-amun). Originally this box must have housed only jewellery made for the king's burial but the inspectors had put into it objects that properly belonged to other boxes.

A third box is shown in Plates 155–156. This stood second in the row to the right of the Anubis pylon, and is in the form of the king's cartouche made of a red-brown wood with borders of ebony veneer. It is incised with inscriptions giving the titularies of the king. The lid is decorated with carved ebony and stained ivory glyphs on a gilt ground giving the nomen of the king. It was found sealed though evidently ransacked by the thieves. It would appear that originally it contained insignia, sceptres and jewels worn by the king in his lifetime and made for him at his coronation.

Sources of the Illustrations

Albert Shoucair, 1, 2, 4, 5, 10, 11, 12, 27, 28, 29, 30, 31, 32, 33, 34, 38, 41, 42, 43, 44, 45, 46, 49, 50, 51, 52, 53, 54, 55, 56, 57, 58, 71, 72, 92, 93, 94, 95, 96, 97, 98, 99, 100, 101, 102, 104, 105, 106, 107, 108, 109, 110, 121, 122, 129, 130, 131, 133, 134, 135, 136, 137, 138, 139, 140; Peter Clayton, 3, 6, 7, 8, 9, 16, 35, 36, 37, 39, 40, 59, 60, 61, 62, 63, 64, 65, 66, 70, 123, 124, 125, 126, 127, 128, 132, 141, 142, 143; courtesy of the Metropolitan Museum of Art, New York,13, 20, 21, 22, 73, 75, 84, 85, 86, 87, 88, 89, 90, 113, 114, 115, 116, 146, 152; courtesy of the Museum of Fine Arts, Boston, 15, 17, 19; Professor Max Hirmer, 18; courtesy of the Brooklyn Museum, New York, 23; Costa, Cairo, 24, 149, 150, 151; courtesy of the Provost and Fellows of Eton College, 25, 26; Tom Scott, Edinburgh, 47, 48, 68, 69, 78, 147; courtesy of the Trustees of the British Museum, 67; courtesy of the Director, Service des Antiquités, Cairo, 74, 76; courtesy of the Walters Art Gallery, Baltimore, 77; courtesy of the Manchester Museum, 79, 80, 81; courtesy of Dr A. Klasens, National Museum of Antiquities, Leyden, 82, 83, 120; courtesy of the Griffith Institute, the Ashmolean Museum, Oxford, 91, 111, 112, 153, 154, 155, 156; F. L. Kenet, copyright George Rainbird Ltd., 1963, 103; Giraudon, Paris, 144, 145; Rosso, Turin, courtesy of Dr Silvio Curto, 117; the author, 119.

Bibliography

The following conventional abbreviations are used to refer to Egyptological publications most frequently cited in the bibliography.

Ann. Serv.	*Annales du Service des Antiquités de l'Egypte*, Cairo
BIFAO	*Bulletin de l'Institut français d'archéologie orientale*, Cairo
BMFA	*Bulletin of the Museum of Fine Arts*, Boston
BMMA	*Bulletin of the Metropolitan Museum of Art*, New York (N.S. New Series)
C.C.G.	*Catalogue général des antiquités égyptiennes du musée du Caire*, Cairo
Chr. d'Eg.	*Chronique d'Egypte*, Brussels
JEA	*Journal of Egyptian Archaeology*, London
ZÄS	*Zeitschrift für Ägyptische Sprache und Altertumskunde*, Leipzig and Berlin

Catalogues and Collections

1 BISSING, FR. W. VON. *Ein thebanischer Grabfund aus dem Anfang des neuen Reichs*, Berlin, 1900.
2 BISSON DE LA ROQUE, F. 'Le Trésor de Tod'. *Chr. d'Eg.* 12 (1937), 20–26.
3 —*Le Trésor de Tod* (*C.C.G.* Nos. 70501–754), Cairo, 1950.
4 BURLINGTON FINE ARTS CLUB. *Catalogue of an Exhibition of Ancient Egyptian Art*, London, 1922.
5 CAIRO MUSEUM. *Brief Guide*, Cairo, 1948.
6 COONEY, J. D. *Five Years of collecting Egyptian Art*, Brooklyn Museum, 1956.
7 EATON, E. S. 'A Group of Middle Kingdom Jewelry'. *BMFA* 29 (1941), 94–8.
8 HAYES, W. C. *The Scepter of Egypt*, 2 vols, New York, 1953–59.
9 HIGGINS, R. A. *Greek and Roman Jewellery*, London, 1961.
10 HOFFMANN, H., and DAVIDSON, P. F. *Greek Gold*, Brooklyn Museum, 1965.
11 MARSHALL, F. H. *Catalogue of the Jewellery, Greek, Etruscan and Roman in the British Museum*, London, 1911.
12 SCHÄFER, H. *Ägyptische Goldschmiedearbeiten*, Berlin Museum, 1910.
13 SCOTT, N. E. 'Egyptian Jewelry'. *BMMA* (N.S.) 22 (1964), 223–34.
14 VERNIER, E. *Bijoux et Orfèvreries* (*C.C.G.* Nos. 52001–53855), 2 vols, Cairo, 1927.
15 VILIMKOVA, M., and ABDUL-RAHMAN, M. H., *Egyptian Jewellery*, London, 1969.
16 WILLIAMS, C. R. *Gold and Silver Jewelry and Related Objects*, New York, 1924.
17 WINLOCK, H. E. *The Treasure of El Lahun*, New York, 1934.
18 —*The Treasure of Three Egyptian Princesses*, New York, 1948.

Excavations and Surveys

19 ALDRED, C. 'Valley Tomb No. 56 at Thebes'. *JEA* 49 (1963), 176–8.
20 BORCHARDT, L. *Das Grabdenkmal des Königs Nefer-ir-ke-Re*, Leipzig, 1909.
21 —*Das Grabdenkmal des Königs Sahu-re*, Leipzig, 1913.
22 —*Excavations at Tell el-Amarna 1913–14* (Annual Report 1915, Smithsonian Institution, Washington, 1916).

23 BRUNTON, G. *Lahun I, the Treasure*, London, 1920.

24 CARTER, H. *et. al. The Tomb of Tutankh-amen*, 3 vols, London, 1923–31.

25 DAVIES, NINA DE G. *Scenes from some Theban Tombs (Private Tombs at Thebes, IV)*, Oxford, 1963.

26 DAVIES, NINA and NORMAN DE G. *The Tombs of Menkheperrasonb, Amenmose and Another*, London, 1933.

27 —*The Tombs of Two Officials of Tuthmosis IV*, London, 1923.

28 DAVIES, NORMAN DE G. *The Rock Tombs of el-Amarna*, 6 vols, London, 1903–8.

29 —'Akhenaten at Thebes'. In *JEA* 9 (1923), 132–52.

30 —*The Tomb of Two Sculptors at Thebes*, New York, 1925.

31 —*The Tomb of Rekh-mi-Re at Thebes*, 2 vols, New York, 1943.

32 DAVIS, T. M., and MASPERO, G. *et. al. The Tomb of Siphtah*, London, 1908.

33 —*et. al. The Tomb of Queen Tiyi*, London, 1910.

34 DE MORGAN, J. *Fouilles à Dahchour, mars-juin 1894*, Vienna, 1895.

35 —*Fouilles à Dahchour en 1894–5*, Vienna, 1903.

36 DESROCHES-NOBLECOURT, C. *Tutankhamen: Life and Death of a Pharaoh*, London, 1963.

37 EDGAR, C. C. 'Report on an Excavation at Toukh el-Qaramous'. *Ann. Serv.* 7 (1907), 206–9.

38 —'The Treasure of Tell Basta'. *Le Musée Egyptien* II, Cairo, 1907, 93–108.

39 ENGELBACH, R. *Riqqeh and Memphis VI*, London, 1915.

40 ENGELBACH, R., and GUNN, B. *Harageh*, London, 1923.

41 FIRTH, C. M. and GUNN, B. *Teti Pyramid Cemeteries (Excavations at Saqqara)*, 2 vols, Cairo, 1926.

42 GONEIM, M. Z. *Horus Sekhemkhet. The Unfinished Step Pyramid at Saqqara*, I, Cairo, 1957.

43 HASSAN, S. *Excavations at Giza*, I-VIII, Oxford and Cairo, 1932–53.

44 MACE, A. C., and WINLOCK, H. E. *The Tomb of Seneb-tisi at Lisht*, New York, 1916.

45 MASPERO, G. 'Le Trésor de Zagazig'. *Revue d'Art Ancien et Moderne*, 23 (1908), 401–12; 24 (1908), 29–38.

46 MONTET, P. *La nécropole de Tanis*, II (*Les Constructions et le tombeau de Psousennès à Tanis*), Paris, 1951.

47 NAVILLE, E. *The Temple of Deir el-Bahari*, 7 vols, London, 1894–1908.

48 PEET, T. E. *Cemeteries of Abydos*, II (1911–12), London, 1914.

49 PETRIE, W. M. F. *The Royal Tombs of the First Dynasty*, London, 1900.

50 —*The Royal Tombs of the Earliest Dynasties*, London, 1901.

51 —*Qurneh*, London, 1909.

52 QUIBELL, J. E. *The Tomb of Yuaa and Thuiu. (C.C.G. Nos. 51001–191)*, Cairo, 1908.

53 QUIBELL, J. E. and HAYTER, A. G. K. *Teti Pyramid, North Side (Excavations at Saqqara)*, Cairo, 1927.

54 REISNER, G. A. *The Early Dynastic Cemeteries of Naga-ed-Der, Pt. I*, Leipzig, 1908.

55 —*Excavations at Kerma*, Cambridge (Mass), 1923.

56 REISNER, G. A. and SMITH, W. S. *The Tomb of Hetep-heres*, Cambridge (Mass), 1955.

57 SÄVE-SÖDERBERGH, T. *Four Eighteenth Dynasty Tombs (Private Tombs at Thebes, Vol. I)*, Oxford, 1957.

58 WINLOCK, H. E. 'The Tombs of the Kings of the Seventeenth Dynasty at Thebes'. *JEA* 10 (1924), 252–5.

59 —*The Tomb of Queen Meryet-Amun at Thebes*, New York, 1932.

60 —*Materials Used at the Embalming of King Tut-ankh-amun*, New York, 1941.

61 —*Excavations at Deir el-Bahri, 1911–31*, New York, 1942.

62 WOOLLEY, C. L. *The Royal Cemetery (Ur Excavations II)*, London, 1934.

Technical Studies

63 CALEY, E. R. *Analyses of Ancient Glasses*, Corning Museum of Glass, New York, 1962.

64 GREAVES, R. H. and LITTLE, O. H. 'Gold Resources of Egypt'. *Report of XVth International Geological Congress*, 1929, 123–7.

65 HARDEN, D. B. *et. al. Masterpieces of Glass*, British Museum, 1968.

66 HARRIS, J. R. *Lexicographical Studies in Ancient Egyptian Minerals*, Berlin, 1961.

67 HARTENBERG, R. C. and SCHMIDT, J. 'The Egyptian Drill and the Origin of the Crank'. *Technology and Culture* 10 (Chicago, 1969), 155ff.

68 JOHNSTON, S. J. *Minerals for Chemical and Allied Industries*, 2nd ed., London, 1961.

69 LINDGREN, W. *Mineral Deposits*, New York, 1928.

70 LUCAS, A. *Ancient Egyptian Materials and Industries*, 3rd ed., London, 1948.

71 MOUSTAFA, A. Y. 'Reparation and Restoration of Antiquities: The Golden Belt of Prince Ptah-Shepses'. *Ann. Serv.* 54 (1957), 149ff.

72 PETRIE, W. M. F. *Arts and Crafts of Ancient Egypt*, 2nd ed., Edinburgh, 1923.

73 PLENDERLEITH, H. J. *The Conservation of Antiquities and Works of Art*, London, 1956.

74 RIEFSTAHL, E. *Ancient Egyptian Glass and Glazes*, Brooklyn Museum, 1968.

75 SINGER, C., HOLMYARD, E. J., HALL, A. R. (editors). *A History of Technology*, I-II, Oxford, 1954–6.

76 VERNIER, E. 'L'Élirage des Fils'. *BIFAO* 12 (1916), 40–41.

77 WOOD, R. W. 'The Purple Gold of Tutankhamun'. *JEA* 20 (1934), 62 ff.

Studies in Design

78 ALDRED, C. 'A Pearl Shell Disk of Ammenemes II'. *JEA* 38 (1952), 130–2.

79 BARGUET, P. 'L'origine et la signification du contrepoids du collier menat'. *BIFAO* 52 (1953), 103–11.

80 BLACKMAN, A. M. 'Philological Notes'. *JEA* 11 (1925), 212–13.

81 BOESER, P. A. A. 'Das Diadem eines der Intef Könige'. *ZÄS* 45 (1908), 30–31.

82 DERCHAIN, P. 'La couroune de la justification'. *Chr. d'Eg.* 30 (1955), 225–87.

83 HAYES, W. C. 'Minor Art and Family History in the Reign of Amunhotpe III'. *BMMA* (N.S.) 6 (1947), 272–9.

84 HIGGINS, R. A. 'Four Greek Rosettes Again'. *British Museum Quarterly* 33 (1969), 112–13.

85 H [ILL], D. K. 'An Egyptian Fish Amulet'. *Bulletin of the Walters Art Gallery, Baltimore* 5 (Nov. 1952), 2.

86 KEIMER, L. 'Pendeloques en Forme d'Insectes'. *Ann. Serv.* 31 (1931), 145–86; 32 (1932), 129–50; 33 (1933), 97–130, 193–200; 34 (1934), 77–213; 36 (1936), 88–114; 37 (1937), 143–72.

87 KERRN, E. E. 'The Development of the Ornamental "Boatman's Fillet" in Old and Middle Kingdom in Egypt'. *Acta Orientalis* 24, 161–8.

88 LACAU, P. *Sarcophages antérieures au nouvel empire.* (*C.C.G.* Nos. 28001–126), 2 vols, Cairo, 1904.

89 MACE, A. C. 'The Caskets of Princess Sit-Hathor-iunut'. *BMMA* 1920, 151–6.

90 MONTET, P. 'Colliers royaux trouvés dans les tombes de Tanis'. *Monuments et Memoirs Piot* 41 (1946), 5–22.

91 MURRAY, M. A. 'Some Pendant Amulets'. *Ancient Egypt* 4 (1917), 49–56.

92 SIMPSON, W. K. 'The Vessels with Engraved Designs . . . from the Tell Basta Treasure'. *American Journal of Archaeology* 63 (1959), 29–45.

93 TROKAY, M. 'Les origines du décor à granulations dans l'orfèvrerie égyptienne'. *Chr. d'Eg.* 43, 1968, 271ff.

94 VERNIER, E. *La Bijouterie et la Joaillerie Égyptiennes*, Cairo, 1907.

95 WINLOCK, H. E. 'Elements from the Dahshur Jewelry'. *Ann. Serv.* 33 (1933), 135-9.

Literary Sources

96 BREASTED, J. H. *Ancient Records of Egypt I-III*, Chicago, 1906.

97 CERNY, J. *Hieratic Inscriptions from the Tomb of Tut-ankh-amun*, Oxford, 1965.

98 DAVIES, N. de G., and MAC-ADAM, M. F. L. *A Corpus of Inscribed Egyptian Funerary Cones*, Oxford, 1957.

99 DIODORUS OF SICILY: trans. by C. H. OLDFATHER (Loeb Edn)., London, 1943.

100 ERMAN, A. (trans. by A. M. Blackman). *The Literature of the Ancient Egyptians*, London, 1927.

101 FAULKNER, R. O. 'Notes on "The Admonitions of an Egyptian Sage" '. *JEA* 50 (1964), 24ff.

102 KNUDTZON, J. A. *Die el-Amarna-Tafeln* 2 vols, Leipzig, 1908, 1915.

103 SETERS, J. VAN. 'A Date for the "Admonitions" in the Second Intermediate Period'. *JEA* 50 (1964), 13ff.

Miscellaneous

104 ALDRED, C. *New Kingdom Art in Ancient Egypt*. 2nd ed., London, 1961.

105 —*Egypt to the End of the Old Kingdom*, London, 1965.

106 BRUYERE, B. 'Un jeune prince ramesside trouvé à Deir el Médineh'. *BIFAO* 25 (1925), 147-65.

107 CAPART, J. GARDINER, A. H. and WALLE, B. VAN DE 'New Light on the Ramesside Tomb Robberies'. *JEA* 22 (1936), 169-93.

108 DAWSON, W. R. 'Deer in Ancient Egypt'. *Journal of the Linnean Society–Zoology* 39 (1934), 137-45.

109 DUSSAUD, R. *L'Art Phénicien du IIieme Millénaire*, Paris, 1949.

110 FISCHER, H. G. 'Cult and Nome of the Goddess Bat'. *Journal of the American Research Center in Egypt* I (1962), 7-24.

111 GARDINER, A. H. *Ancient Egyptian Onomastica*. 3 vols, Oxford, 1947.

112 HAYES, W. C. 'Daily Life in Ancient Egypt'. *National Geographic Magazine* 80 (Oct. 1941), 466.

113 JAMES, T. G. H. 'Egypt from the Expulsion of the Hyksos to Amenophis I'. *Cambridge Ancient History* 2nd ed., Vol. II, Ch. VIII, Cambridge, 1965.

114 LANGE, K. and HIRMER, H. *Egypt: Architecture, Sculpture and Painting*, London, 1956.

115 MEKHITARIAN, A. *Egyptian Paintings*, Geneva, 1954.

116 SETHE, K. 'Hitherto Unnoticed Evidence regarding Copper Works of Art'. *JEA* I (1914), 233-6.

117 SMITH, W. S. *A History of Egyptian Sculpture and Painting in the Old Kingdom*. Boston, (Mass), 1949.

118 —*The Art and Architecture of Ancient Egypt*. 2nd ed., Harmondsworth, 1965.

Notes on the Text

References preceded by *Bibl.* are to the numbered list in the Bibliography, p. 246.

CHAPTER ONE

1 *Bibl.* 107, 169ff.
2 *Bibl.* 18, 8–9.
3 *Bibl.* 58, 252–5.
4 *Bibl.* 34 and 35.
5 *Bibl.* 23.
6 *Bibl.* 17.
7 *Bibl.* 7, 97—8.
8 *Bibl.* 112.
9 *Bibl.* 32.
10 *Bibl.* 19.
11 *Bibl.* 46, 135–58, 167–72.
12 *Bibl.* 45 and 38.
13 *Bibl.* 37.

CHAPTER TWO

1 *Bibl.* 5, No. 6076.
2 *Bibl.* 97, 11–12, No. 52.
3 *Bibl.* 103, 13–23.
4 *Bibl.* 101, 25, ref. 3, 2.
5 *Bibl.* 21, 60–4, 121.
6 *Bibl.* 96, i § 372.
7 *Bibl.* 117, 171–2.
8 *Bibl.* 96, ii § 23.
9 *Bibl.* 113, § v.
10 *Bibl.* 96, ii § 23.
11 *Bibl.* 102, Nos. 22, 25.
12 *Ibid*, Nos. 10, 11, 14.
13 *Bibl.* 83.
14 *Bibl.* 8, i fig. 27.

CHAPTER THREE

1 *Bibl.* 64.
2 *Bibl.* 96, iii§§ 170–1, 175–6, 195, 286 §§ 289–90.
3 *Bibl.* 31, 26, Pl. xviii.
4 *Bibl.* 99, iii, 12–14.
5 *Bibl.* 96, iii §195.
6 *Bibl.* 70, 277–8.
7 *Bibl.* 66, 35–6.
8 *Bibl.* 102, No. 7, ll. 69–72, No. 10, ll. 19–20.
9 *Bibl.* 9, 3–4, 6.
10 *Bibl.* 72, 94.
11 *Bibl.* 77, 62–5.
12 *Bibl.* 73, 208–9.
13 *Bibl.* 102, No. 22, i, ll. 20, 25, ii; ll. 8, 15.
14 *Bibl.* 36, Pl. xxiia.
15 *Cf. Bibl.* 66, 50.
16 *Bibl.* 70, 546, Nos. 1, 2, 3.
17 *Bibl.* 2, 20–6.
18 *Bibl.* 97, 87, §47.
19 *Bibl.* 90, 19.
20 Pap. Hood (B.M. 10202), *Bibl.* 111, i, 68★, No. 162.
21 *Bibl.* 70, 451.
22 *Ibid*, 450.
23 *Ibid*, 445.
24 *Ibid*, 447, 459.
25 *Bibl.* 74, 2; and 70, 393–4.
26 *Bibl.* 61, 46.
27 *Bibl.* 70, 252–3.
28 *Bibl.* 65, 11; and 70, 217.
29 *Bibl.* 66, 100.
30 *Ibid*, 24.

CHAPTER FOUR

1 *Bibl.* 100, 68.
2 *Bibl.* 53, 32–6.
3 *Bibl.* 29, 136 ff. and 28, vi 1–6.
4 *Bibl.* 92, 43–4.
5 *Viz.* Tombs Nos. 114, 169, 189.
6 *Bibl.* 98, Nos. 160, 220, 266, 467, 533.
7 *Viz.* Tombs Nos. 140, 165.
8 *Bibl.* 16, 4 and note 21.
9 *Bibl.* 30, 57–8, Pl. xi.
10 *Bibl.* 26, Pls. x, xi; and 27, Pls. vii, viii.
11 *Bibl.* 52, vii.
12 *Bibl.* 96, ii §975.
13 See Chapter Three, note 20.
14 *Bibl.* 66, 23–4.
15 *Bibl.* 16, 2 note 10. *Cf. Bibl.* 102, No. 29, ll. 34, 39.
16 *Bibl.* 75, i figs. 382–3.
17 *Bibl.* 8, ii fig. 129.

CHAPTER FIVE

1 *Bibl.* 96, ii §867.
2 *Bibl.* 109, 19.
3 *Bibl.* 92, 31.
4 *Bibl.* 70, 262.
5 *Bibl.* 10, 25.
6 *Bibl.* 22, 453–4, Pls. 7–8.
7 *Bibl.* 9, 31; and 10, 34.
8 *Bibl.* 116, 233–5.
9 *Bibl.* 10, 36.
10 *Bibl.* 84, 112–3.
11 *Bibl.* 12, 14 note 1, 26 No. 2; *Bibl.* 94, 58–62; *Bibl.* 76, 40–1.
12 I am indebted to Miss Nora Scott of the Metropolitan Museum for this information.
13 *Bibl.* 9, 14–16.
14 *Bibl.* 70, 248.
15 *Bibl.* 40, 14–15, Pl. xxii, 5.
16 See Chapter Three, note 10.
17 *Bibl.* 68, 90 and 69, 341.
18 *Bibl.* 62, 296.

19 *Bibl.* 9, 36.
20 *Bibl.* 10, 43.
21 British Patent No. 415181, March 1933.
22 *Bibl.* 10, 46.
23 *Ibid*, 47 note 67.
24 *Bibl.* 70, 248.
25 *Bibl.* 10, 36–8.
26 *Bibl.* 18, 23, Pl. xliia.
27 *Bibl.* 56, 43–4; and 86, 34 (1934), 194.
28 *Bibl.* 62, Pl. 138 (U. 10409), Pls. 151–2.
29 *Bibl.* 20, 59–66, Pls i, iii.
30 *Bibl.* 41, Pl. 15, B5.
31 *Bibl.* 70, 283.
32 *Bibl.* 14, No. 52658.
33 Such a technique has been used to cast the statuette of Tuthmosis IV (*c.* 1414 BC) in the British Museum (No. 64564) according to an unpublished report of the Museum Laboratory.
34 *Bibl.* 8, ii fig. 129.
35 *Ibid.*
36 *Bibl.* 16, 9.
37 *Bibl.* 55, 93–4.
38 *Bibl.* 67, 155.
39 *Bibl.* 70, 55.
40 *Bibl.* 31, 49 note 21.
41 *Bibl.* 70, 179.
42 *Ibid.*
43 *Ibid*, 56.
44 *Bibl.* 55, 91–2; and 72, 118–9.
45 *Ibid*, 125.
46 *Bibl.* 65, 11.
47 *Bibl.* 70, 13.
48 *Bibl.* 75, ii 312–3.
49 *Bibl.* 70, 218, 219.

50 The writer's observations are based upon enlargements of photographs in the Carter archives of the Ashmolean Museum, Oxford.

CHAPTER SIX

1 *Bibl.* 44, 58–9, 87; and 161–8.
2 *Bibl.* 82, 225–87.
3 *Bibl.* 87, 176, 187.
4 *Bibl.* 117, fig. 64.
5 *Bibl.* 6, No. 21.
6 *Bibl.* 25, Pl. vi (interpreted as a collar).
7 *Bibl.* 59, 14, figs. 1, 2 (*cf.* Pl. xvii).
8 *Bibl.* 80, 212–3.
9 *Bibl.* 100, 38–40.
10 *Bibl.* 106, 157–62.
11 *Bibl.* 16, 116.
12 *Bibl.* 62, Pls. 129, 138, 145, 146.
13 *Bibl.* 51, 6–10.
14 *Bibl.* 18, 17–18; and 16, 116.
15 *Bibl.* 8, ii fig. 102.
16 *Bibl.* 52, Pl. lix.
17 *Ibid*, Pl. lviii.
18 *Bibl.* 24, iii 74–5.
19 *Bibl.* 28, iv Pl. xxxi.
20 *Bibl.* 8, ii 252.
21 *Bibl.* 33, Pl. xxxiii.
22 *Bibl.* 118, Pls. 117, 131.
23 *Bibl.* 61, 111, Pl. 87.
24 *Bibl.* 48, 47 (S.29), Pl. ix, fig. 4; and 11, No. 1593, fig. 48.
25 *Bibl.* 44, 62–3.
26 *Bibl.* 88, Pl. li, Nos. 430–3.
27 *Bibl.* 44, 65.

28 *Bibl.* 24, ii 120–4.
29 *Bibl.* 88, Pl. lii, Nos. 439–43; *ibid*, Pls. lxxix-lxxxi, and 88 etc.
30 *Ibid*, Pl. liii, Nos. 462–7 and 91.
31 *Bibl.* 110, 11–15.
32 *Bibl.* 78, 130–2.
33 *Bibl.* 40, Pl. xv, 2.
34 *Bibl.* 8, i, 220.
35 *Bibl.* 115, 51.
36 *Bibl.* 8, i 148, fig. 153; and 40, Pl. xv, 5.
37 *Bibl.* 104, No. 1.
38 *Bibl.* 17, 51.
39 *Bibl.* 14, No. 52074 and 8, ii fig. 100.
40 *Bibl.* 57, Pl. xxx.
41 *Bibl.* 28, iii Pl. iii.
42 *Bibl.* 17, 53.
43 *Ibid*, 51.
44 *Bibl.* 58, 261, Pl. xvii.
45 *Bibl.* 14, No. 52069.
46 *Ibid*, No. 52577; and 32, 39–40.
47 *Bibl.* 114, Pl. 212. *Cf.* figure of the god Amun at Deir el-Bahri (and 47, iv, Pl. cid) which is a Ramessid restoration.
48 *Bibl.* 17, 49 and 18, 31–2.
49 *Bibl.* 24, ii, 136, Pl. lxxxii b.
50 *Bibl.* 7, 94–8.
51 *Bibl.* 8, ii 185–6.
52 *Ibid*, 396–7.
53 *Bibl.* 14, Nos. 52, 238–9.
54 *Bibl.* 24, i Pl. xxxviii.
55 *Bibl.* 71, 149ff. and 15, Pls. 7–8.
56 *Bibl.* 44, 17, 38, Pl. xx.
57 *Bibl.* 16, 47–54; and 18, 26–7.

Index

Numbers in italics refer to the plates